Advanced Interpersonal Communication

Student Manual

Advanced Interpersonal Communication

Series Product Managers:	Charles G. Blum and Adam A. Wilcox
Developmental Editor:	Michelle Togut
Project Editor:	Josh Pincus
Series Designer:	Adam A. Wilcox

Trademarks

Disclaimer

Student Manual: ISBN-10 = 0-619-07599-6 / ISBN-13 = 978-0-619-07599-6

Student Manual + CBT: ISBN-10 = 1-4188-4566-3 / ISBN-13 = 978-1-4188-4566-7

Printed in the United States of America

1 2 3 4 5 6 7 8 9 10 GL 10 09 08

Contents

Advanced Interpersonal Communication

Introduction

After reading this introduction, you will know how to:

A Use ILT Series training manuals in general.

B Use prerequisites, a target student description, course objectives, and a skills inventory to properly set your expectations for the course.

Topic A: About the manual

ILT Series philosophy

ILT Series training manuals facilitate your learning by providing structured interaction with the subject matter. While we provide text to explain difficult concepts, the hands-on activities are the focus of our courses. By paying close attention as your instructor leads you through these activities, you will learn the skills and concepts effectively.

We believe strongly in the instructor-led classroom. During class, focus on your instructor. Our manuals are designed and written to facilitate your interaction with your instructor, and not to call attention to manuals themselves.

We believe in the basic approach of setting expectations, delivering instruction, and providing summary and review afterwards. For this reason, lessons begin with objectives and end with summaries. We also provide overall course objectives and a course summary to provide both an introduction to and closure on the entire course.

Manual components

The manuals contain these major components:

- Table of contents
- Introduction
- Units
- Course summary
- Glossary
- Index

Each element is described below.

Table of contents

The table of contents acts as a learning roadmap.

Introduction

The introduction contains information about our training philosophy and our manual components, features, and conventions. It contains target student, prerequisite, objective, and setup information for the specific course.

Units

Units are the largest structural component of the course content. A unit begins with a title page that lists objectives for each major subdivision, or topic, within the unit. Within each topic, conceptual and explanatory information alternates with hands-on activities. Units conclude with a summary comprising one paragraph for each topic, and an independent practice activity that gives you an opportunity to practice the skills you've learned.

The conceptual information takes the form of text paragraphs, exhibits, lists, and tables. The activities are structured in two columns, one telling you what to do, the other providing explanations, descriptions, and graphics.

Course summary

This section provides a text summary of the entire course. It is useful for providing closure at the end of the course. The course summary also indicates the next course in this series, if there is one, and lists additional resources you might find useful as you continue to learn about the software.

Glossary

The glossary provides definitions of key terms used in the course.

Index

The index enables you to quickly find information about a particular feature or concept of the software.

Manual conventions

We've tried to keep the number of elements and the types of formatting to a minimum in the manuals. This aids in clarity and makes the manuals more classically elegant looking. But there are some conventions and icons you should know about.

Convention/Icon	Description
Italic text	In conceptual text, indicates a new term or feature.
Bold text	In unit summaries, indicates a key term or concept. In an independent practice activity, indicates an explicit item that you select, choose, or type.
`Code font`	Indicates code or syntax.
Select **bold item**	In the left column of hands-on activities, bold sans-serif text indicates an explicit item that you select, choose, or type.
Keycaps like e	Indicate a key on the keyboard you must press.

Activities

The activities are the most important parts of our manuals. They are usually divided into two columns, with a questions or concepts on the left and answers and explanations on the right. Here's a sample:

Do it!

A-1:   Steps for brainstorming

Exercises
1 Sequence the steps for brainstorming.
Begin generating ideas.
Select the purpose.
Organize for the session.
Ask questions and clarify ideas.
Review the rules.

Topic B: Setting your expectations

Properly setting your expectations is essential to your success. This topic will help you do that by providing:

- A description of the target student at whom the course is aimed
- A list of the objectives for the course
- A skills assessment for the course

Target student

The typical students of this course will be managers, supervisors, or team leaders who want to improve their communication skills to communicate more effectively with subordinates, superiors, colleagues, customers, or vendors in order to improve their job performance and enhance employee morale.

Course objectives

These overall course objectives will give you an idea about what to expect from the course. It is also possible that they will help you see that this course is not the right one for you. If you think you either lack the prerequisite knowledge or already know most of the subject matter to be covered, you should let your instructor know that you think you are misplaced in the class.

After completing this course, you will know how to:

- Interact with individuals who display a specific communication style and communicate using various verbal and nonverbal modes of communication.
- Identify the elements that influence first impressions, build rapport and establish credibility with others, and build positive relationships.
- Use paraphrasing effectively and provide positive and constructive feedback in a business setting.
- Identify the types of ineffective supervisors and use different techniques to deal with them, and identify the steps necessary to prepare for negotiating a raise and to resign a job.
- Identify the guidelines for communicating with colleagues, take appropriate steps to apologize to a subordinate, and use appropriate tactics to refuse a subordinate's request.
- Respond to customers' complaints and identify a proper way to reject a vendor's contract without rejecting the vendor.
- Determine the nature of an organization's culture, use the cultural network to your advantage and identify the characteristics of the roles exhibited in a cultural network, select the elements of physical culture that affect interpersonal communication, and identify the ways in which managers can build a positive culture.

Skills inventory

Use the following form to gauge your skill level entering the class. For each skill listed, rate your familiarity from 1 to 5, with five being the most familiar. *This is not a test.* Rather, it is intended to provide you with an idea of where you're starting from at the beginning of class. If you're wholly unfamiliar with all the skills, you might not be ready for the class. If you think you already understand all of the skills, you might need to move on to the next Module in the series. In either case, you should let your instructor know as soon as possible.

Skill	1	2	3	4	5
Interact with individuals who display a specific primary communication style					
Interact with individuals who display a specific secondary communication style					
Identify types of nonverbal communication					
Influence a first impression					
Build rapport with others					
Establish credibility with others					
Ask effective questions					
Avoid certain types of questions					
Identify different forms of feedback					
Use paraphrasing					
Provide positive feedback					
Provide constructive feedback					
Handle different types of ineffective supervisors					
Negotiate a raise with supervisor					
Submit a resignation					
Communicate with colleagues					

Skill	1	2	3	4	5
Apologize to subordinates					
Dismiss a subordinate					
Respond to customer complaints					
Complain to a vendor					
Identify elements of an organizational culture					
Identify roles exhibited in the cultural network					
Identify elements of physical culture					
Create a supportive climate					

Topic C: Reviewing the course

This section describes the setup instructions for reviewing this course.

Course review setup

There are no special setup instructions for reviewing this course.

Unit 1

Communication styles and methods

Unit time: 45 minutes

Complete this unit, and you'll know how to:

A Identify primary and secondary communication styles.

B Communicate using various verbal and nonverbal modes of communication.

Topic A: Communication styles

Explanation

To be successful in the workplace, you must be able to effectively communicate and cooperate with clients and co-workers. Learning about the four types of communication styles helps a listener understand a speaker's perspective and a speaker understand how his or her communication affects the listener.

By understanding different communication styles, you can expedite interactions between people because you will not need to repeat, define, and analyze each sentence or phrase. Such understanding affects a company's bottom line. Miscommunication costs companies by causing errors, and misunderstanding costs companies by slowing the production of goods or services.

Primary communication styles

There are four types of communication styles, of which no one style is better than another. The population is equally divided among the four styles, and each serves an important role in the workplace. The four primary communication styles are:

- Collaborator
- Contributor
- Inquisitor
- Director

Collaborator

Collaborators are approachable because they are friendly and open. They thrive on interactions with people, have high-energy levels, and are outgoing. Because of their enthusiasm, they are usually good motivators and expect others to be just as enthusiastic about each of their new ideas. As a result, co-workers occasionally see collaborators as impulsive.

While people who fall into this group are often called visionaries, many times they are so full of new ideas that they might not have time to finish work on their previous projects. When communicating, collaborators are expert storytellers. The collaborator tends to be dramatic and will cite examples or tell stories before quoting statistics, unless the statistics are sensational. When it comes to offering opinions, the collaborator is apt to be straightforward. They often "think out loud" and skip from topic to topic without a logical path. Collaborators expect chitchat and see it as a critical part of building rapport in the workplace.

Contributor

Contributors are socially oriented, but prefer speaking with people in small groups or individually. Contributors are good listeners and are open to opinions and new ideas. Often, contributors are masters at the art of compromise and are called upon to be the peacemaker in group settings. However, contributors' diplomacy leads them to be viewed as indecisive and non-authoritarian. In addition, their desire to maintain a peaceful environment might lead contributors to repress angry feelings. Instead, they might air their complaints to a third party. When this happens, contributors are not seeking advice or resolution but want someone to listen as they release the anger they have kept hidden.

Inquisitor

Inquisitors are the perfectionists of communication. Logic and reason rule the communication of an inquisitor. Generally, both the phrasing and repercussions of any question or response that an inquisitor gives have been well thought out. The inquisitor does not typically speak in emotional terms but prefers data and hard facts. Inquisitors like to minimize risk through strict attention to detail. Unfortunately, the inquisitors' high standards often lead people to view them as overly critical of themselves and others. Inquisitors like small groups or one-on-one interactions but prefer to work alone.

Director

Directors focus on the completion of tasks. Most directors adopt a practical approach to situations and generally take action when someone with a different communication style is still analyzing or planning. This gives directors a reputation for being decisive; however, they can change their opinions, sometimes radically, when they perceive that a situation has changed. Occasionally, directors' decisiveness and quick action can be frustrating to others, especially in situations where the quick decision was the wrong one. In addition, because directors tend to be forthright with opinions and reach their points quickly, their communication style can be intimidating. Often, directors are perceived as lacking compassion, but they frequently express support through action rather than empathy.

Do it!

A-1: Identifying primary communication styles

Exercises

1 Watch the movie clip and then answer the following questions.

Who in the given discussion is a collaborator?

Was Phyllis able to get across her idea?

2 Watch the movie clip and then answer the following questions.

What is Brett's communication style?

How did Brett feel?

3 In the following scene, Carlene (supervisor) and Pam (subordinate) are seated at the table in Carlene's office.

Carlene: You were awfully quiet in the meeting, Pam. I wanted to give you a chance to share your opinions with me.

Pam: Well, I've reviewed both options, and I really think that Terry's plan was the best. Sonya gave us lots of information but not a lot of facts about the effects of her proposal. With Terry's plan, we know exactly where we stand at all times.

Carlene: Would you be more willing to consider Sonya's suggestions if you had more data?

Pam: Yes, probably. It sounded like a workable plan, but there just weren't any facts to support it.

Which communication style does
Pam demonstrate?

Did Pam consider facts and data
when making a decision?

Why do you think Pam did not volunteer her opinions in the meeting?

4 In the following scene, John (subordinate) and Phyllis (supervisor) are seated at the table in John's office.

John: ...and that's why I've decided to go with Sonya's proposal.

Phyllis: How does your team feel about that?

John: There's some opposition, but I'm sure I can win them over. Sonya's proposal really is the best.

Phyllis: You're confident of that?

John: Well, as confident as I can be, I guess. Her presentation was the best, and besides, we need to go ahead and get started on stage two of the plan. Time is money, you know.

Which communication style does
John demonstrate?

What are the characteristics of
John's communication style?

5 What is your communication
style?

6 On the right side, explain how you would deal with each of the following
communications styles

Collaborator

Contributor

Inquisitor

Director

Secondary communication styles

Explanation

When under stress, most people display a secondary communication style that is determined by the primary communication style. Although they vary widely in other attributes, the main characteristic of the secondary styles is inflexibility. There are four secondary communication styles:

- Aggressor
- Consenter
- Avoider
- Controller

Aggressor

Acting aggressively is the collaborator's secondary communication style. Although collaborators are normally people-oriented, they often express their frustrations by verbally attacking others. Belligerence, a loud voice, and emphatic language and gestures characterize aggressive communication. Fortunately, outbursts are rare and usually subside fairly quickly. Once collaborators have vented their frustration, they are ready to put the incident behind them.

Consenter

The contributor's secondary communication style is to consent. Contributors are peacemakers, and that characteristic is taken to the extreme when under duress. Contributors become inflexible and unwilling to discuss any problems or situations that might be responsible for their stress. Although outwardly cooperative, contributors show subtle forms of disagreement and frustration in their body language and behavior. Contributors are slow to anger, but they are also slow to forgive and forget.

Avoider

Avoidance is the inquisitor's secondary communication style. Normally quiet and reserved, inquisitors cope with stress by avoiding all emotional expression and contact with others. If emotional withdrawal is ineffective, inquisitors might physically remove themselves from situations.

Controller

Controlling is the director's secondary communication style. Directors are naturally determined, so they become very controlling when under duress. Exercising control over the people around them allows directors to feel that they have control over situations. Whatever emotion a director might normally show is lost when controlling, and he becomes completely focused on obtaining a specific goal. The already rapid pace of directors' decision-making processes becomes even more rapid when they are under stress, which frustrates people who have other communication styles.

Do it!

A-2: Identifying secondary communication styles

Exercises

1 Identify the four secondary communication styles.

   A   Aggressor, Consenter, Avoider, Controller

   B   Collaborator, Communicator, Inquisitor, Demander

   C   Collaborator, Contributor, Inquisitor, Director

   D   Communicator, Consenter, Avoider, Demander

2 Which of the following is a director's secondary communication style?

   A   Avoider

   B   Controller

   C   Consenter

   D   Aggressor

3 What is your secondary style of communication?

Topic B: Verbal and nonverbal communication

Explanation

Effective communication involves both verbal and nonverbal techniques. How you use your voice says a great deal about you. Listeners take note of your vocal characteristics and form opinions about your sincerity, enthusiasm, and even your knowledge of the topic being discussed. Your body language also clues listeners into your state of mind. Your posture, the firmness of your handshake, and your willingness to make eye contact all tell listeners something about your personality and character. You need to make sure you're communicating the same message with both your voice and your body language.

Verbal communication

Your voice often indicates whether you are nervous, which might affect how a listener perceives your credibility. Being able to control your voice and communicate in a pleasing way attracts and maintains listeners' attention. There are three vocal characteristics you can control to become a more effective speaker: volume, rate, and pitch.

Volume is a vocal characteristic you need to tailor to the environment. Room size, number of listeners, and external noise all influence the volume of your voice. Make sure your listeners can hear everything you say.

Rate is the speed at which you speak. Every person has a different natural rate, so it is important to adapt your rate to the topic and listener. Nervous speakers tend to speak rapidly. If you feel anxious about the message you are delivering, you should try to maintain a slow, even rate of speech, so that the listener hears the actual message instead of being distracted by your nervousness. Conversely, you should not let your speaking rate drop much below 120 words per minute, or you risk losing the listener's attention. Stay enthusiastic about your message to maintain an appropriate rate.

Pitch is the highness or lowness of your voice. When your vocal muscles are taut, your voice has a high pitch; when your vocal muscles are relaxed, your voice has a low pitch. If you are nervous, your vocal muscles will tighten and your voice will rise above its natural pitch.

Rate and volume also affect your pitch. When you speak rapidly, your muscles are tense, which causes your pitch to rise. Speaking loudly also causes your pitch to rise. Although pitch variations might be useful in emphasizing certain points, generally it is best to maintain an even and natural pitch in most situations.

Positive language

Positive language draws both the speaker and the listener into a conversation. It presents an all-inclusive attitude and makes all parties feel empowered. A speaker can use positive language to show that he or she has confidence in her message. Positive language includes phrases such as "we can" and "we will."

Negative language

Negative language can be expressed in a variety of ways, but the main concern with negative language is the word "no." The word "no" delivers a blunt, end-of-conversation attitude, regardless of the rest of the message. If at all possible, avoid using the word "no" and any other negative language such as "can't," "won't," and "don't."

Inflammatory language

Inflammatory language is meant to stir intense negative emotions in the listener. It is often prejudicial against someone because of gender, ethnicity, or physical attributes. Inflammatory language is always inappropriate in the workplace.

Powerful language

Powerful language involves the use of clear, direct statements of fact and feeling rather than dancing around an issue. A powerful speaker lets you know exactly what the situation is and how to handle it efficiently and effectively.

A powerless speaker uses "hedge phrases," such as, "I guess…"and "Maybe we should…." Often, powerless speakers form their ideas as questions, such as, "Shouldn't we start the meeting?" instead of stating, "We should start the meeting." Powerless speakers tend to be disappointed with the results of their ambiguity.

Keep in mind that speaking powerfully does not mean being blunt, abrupt, or rude. An effective powerful speaker combines politeness with directness so as to be clear and concise.

Do it!

B-1:   Using verbal communication

Multiple-choice questions

1 Identify the characteristics of negative language.

   A   Dull, discourages conversation

   B   Bold, encourages conversation

   C   Blunt, ends conversation

   D   Timid, ends conversation

2 Which of the following phrases defines inflammatory language?

   A   Inflammatory language is appropriate and insignificant.

   B   Inflammatory language stirs negative emotions and is prejudicial.

   C   Inflammatory language is angry and prejudicial.

   D   Inflammatory language is intense and always appropriate.

Nonverbal communication

Explanation

You are constantly communicating with those around you. You express fear, anger, happiness, sadness, enthusiasm, and many other emotions without even saying a word. It is important to be aware of the signals you are communicating to those around you. It is also important to be able to recognize the nonverbal signals that others are communicating to you.

When meeting with someone, nonverbal communication gives each of you clues about the other's personality, attitudes, and feelings. The five types of nonverbal communication that have the most impact on your conversations are:

- Handshakes
- Expression and eye contact
- Proximity
- Touch
- Gestures and posture

Handshake

A firm handshake is the foundation of any business interaction. Some people carry firmness to the extreme; it is not the same thing as tightly squeezing. On the other hand, you do not want to give a "cold fish" handshake. A good firm handshake starts with a dry palm; carry a handkerchief if you need to wipe damp palms before entering a meeting where you expect to shake someone's hand. Grasp the other person's palm, not just the fingers. To capture that person's attention, hold onto his hand for just a second longer than feels natural, and begin talking before you let go to further maintain his attention.

Expression and eye contact

A friendly expression and direct eye contact send a message that you are open, honest, and enthusiastic. When coming into a meeting or interaction, smile and look into the eyes of the other person as you are introduced. You can show interest in the other person by maintaining eye contact as she speaks. When you tilt your head toward the speaker, you give the impression that you are an interested listener. These cues encourage the other person to relax and help open the lines of communication.

Proximity

Personal space is an important element to keep in mind when communicating. Typically, people of a higher status tend to keep more than the normal four to six feet between themselves and their subordinates. Close friends and romantic partners usually keep approximately 18 inches of distance. While you do not want to give the appearance of invading an acquaintance's personal space, too great a distance will send a message that you are not totally involved in the conversation. Three to five feet of distance will evoke feelings of closeness, trust, and parallel status between acquaintances.

Touch

Touch in the workplace must be dealt with carefully. Touching in the workplace is more common between women than men. Appropriate touching can convey openness, trustworthiness, and interest. It also can result in self-disclosure and compliance. Appropriate touching includes a light touch on the shoulder or arm of an acquaintance or a handshake.

Inappropriate touching conveys disrespect to the recipient of the touch. It might also demonstrate hostility. Inappropriate touching includes lingering contact and caresses. When determining the appropriateness of a touch, you should also consider the pressure that was used in the touch, the body part that did the touching, what body part received the touch, and if anyone else was present when contact was made.

Gestures and posture

Although most people are aware of the hand gestures that flow naturally throughout the course of communication, many people are less aware of the messages that hand, leg, and foot activity send. Restless hands or legs can suggest nervousness, which might make people question your honesty or integrity. Fidgeting might also indicate impatience and concealed anger. To ease nervousness, take deep, calming breaths and practice keeping your hands, feet, and legs still.

Similarly, your posture can affect the impression you make on someone. Standing and sitting straight signals that you are ready for open communication. Sitting or standing hunched over gives the impression that you are uninterested in conversation or contact.

Do it!

B-2: Using nonverbal communication methods

Exercises
1 Which of the following are types of nonverbal communication.
A   Charisma
B   Handshake
C   Proximity
D   Touch
E   Intelligence
F   Gestures and Posture
G   Expression and Eye Contact

2 What messages do the following pictures convey?

3 Your instructor will choose one student to play the role of a person who has just taken over as Interim Director of Industrial Casing Products. This person has the task of reducing the number of different styles of cases manufactured, and now has to meet with the Sales Manager of Industrial Casing Products.

The Interim Director must discuss the option of reducing the number of styles with the Sales Manager, as well as announce his appointment to the position of Interim Director of Casing Products.

The Sales Manager is task-oriented and confident. While practical when addressing day-to-day situations, this manager can be impatient and insensitive to others, and always wants to be in control of a situation. In addition, the Sales Manager is not considered a good team player.

What communication style did the Sales Manager use during the discussion?

What communication style did Interim Director use during the discussion?

What went right during the discussion?

Unit summary: Communication styles and methods

Topic A

In this unit, you learned about the different communication styles. You learned that there are four **primary types: collaborator, contributor, inquisitor,** and **director**. You also learned that there are **secondary styles** associated with each of these: **aggressor, consenter, avoider**, and **controller**.

Topic B

Finally, you learned about the different **verbal and nonverbal modes** of communication. You learned that **tone, pitch, and volume as well as language** affect communication, and that nonverbal cues, such as **gestures, eye contact, proximity, and touch**, can communicate your feelings to others.

Independent practice activity

1 Identify the four secondary communication styles.

    A Communicator, Consenter, Interrogator, Demander

    B Collaborator, Contributor, Inquisitor, Director

    C Aggressor, Consenter, Avoider, Controller

    D Collaborator, Consenter, Inquisitor, Director

2 What are the characteristics of negative language?

3 Which of the following phrases best defines inflammatory language?

    A Inflammatory language is intense and non-prejudicial.

    B Inflammatory language is angry and prejudicial.

    C Inflammatory language stirs negative emotions and is prejudicial.

    D Inflammatory language is prejudicial and always appropriate.

4 People with which communication style prefer to speak in a small group?

    A Contributor

    B Collaborator

    C Inquisitor

    D Director

5 Which of the following communication styles is friendly and open?

A Contributor

B Collaborator

C Inquisitor

D Director

6 Which of the following is the secondary communication style of a collaborator?

A Aggressor

B Controller

C Consenter

D Avoider

7 What message do you communicate when you make direct eye contact with a person to whom you are speaking?

Unit 2

First impressions and building rapport

Unit time: 40 minutes

Complete this unit, and you'll know how to:

A Identify the elements that influence a first impression.

B Build rapport and establish credibility with others.

C Build positive relationships.

Topic A: The importance of first impressions

Explanation   Although it only takes 30 to 45 seconds to formulate a first impression, it often requires four or five additional encounters to change someone's first impression. Many times, once you've made a first impression, you will not have a second opportunity to change that impression. Therefore, it's important to make your best impression on the first try.

Elements influencing first impressions

Physical elements such as posture and attire can influence the impression you make, but often impressions are based on abstract qualities such as:

- Appearance
- Knowledge
- Social composure

Appearance

Your appearance is comprised of several factors: the clothes you wear, your personal hygiene, your posture, and even your handshake all leave impressions on people you meet. When meeting people for the first time, it is best to do some research and find out about their environment. If you are entering a different country or culture, determine whether your attire is appropriate. Learn how that culture views eye contact—some cultures consider downcast eyes to be a sign of dishonesty while others see it as a sign of respect. Discover what hand gestures are considered inappropriate or rude, and avoid them.

Even if you are not meeting in a new environment, you might feel concerned about the appropriateness of your attire. If possible, find out before the meeting how the other person or people will be dressed and match their style. If you are visiting a corporation on a "casual Friday," ask what the dress code is. To some companies, casual means employees can wear slacks and loafers; to other companies, casual means jeans and tennis shoes. Do your best to duplicate the styles and characteristics of the people in your meeting environment so messages will not be cluttered by misperception.

Knowledge

Although your intelligence will not be scored in a business meeting, it will be tested and judged based on your competence. You are expected to have a thorough understanding of the subject of your meeting, particularly if you are giving a presentation. Just as you would research different cultures in order to adapt to them beforehand, so too should you research the topic of your meeting beforehand. This will prepare you to answer any questions that arise. If you do not know the answer to a question, do not lie. Rather, admit that you do not know the answer and promise to find out. Then, make sure to follow through on that promise. Let the person know when you'll be able to provide her with an answer, and deliver it at that time.

Social composure

Social composure comprises grace, charm, and etiquette. Being graceful in a meeting or social activity involves being comfortable in your surroundings. Knowing that you are appropriately attired and are familiar with the customs and culture of your group will help put you at ease. Simply being friendly is the key to exhibiting charm. You can build rapport with your associates by listening to and sharing with them. Be sure your communication involves a two-way exchange of information. Displaying the proper etiquette for the environment will also lead you toward achieving a high level of social composure. Being polite to your associates will communicate a desire to build rapport.

Do it!

A-1:   Identifying elements of a first impression

Exercises

1 Identify the elements that influence first impressions.

   A   Friendship

   B   Word choice

   C   Appearance

   D   Social composure

   E   Expression

   F   Knowledge

2 Below are two images. What is your first impression of person A and person B. Whom would you like to meet again for a professional interaction?

Person A

Person B

3 Why do you think that the campaign shown below failed in Arabic countries?

Topic B: Communicating to build rapport

Explanation

Rapport is a relationship of mutual trust. In any relationship, it is necessary for you to gain and maintain a sense of trust so that you can to communicate freely with one another. Without trust, communication is superficial at best and nonexistent at worst. You also need to establish your credibility to communicate effectively, which means you need to ensure that listeners respect and believe you.

Rapport

Building rapport is an ongoing process that begins when you have your first encounter. There are three guidelines you should follow to build rapport:

- Adapt to the other person's communication style.
- Find common ground with the other person.
- Focus on mutually beneficial goals.

Adapt to the other person's communication style

By paying attention to conversation and body language, you should be able to determine the other person's primary communication style. Recognizing a person's communication style allows you to adapt your own communication style to his so that the two of you are compatible.

For example, if you determine that you are speaking with an inquisitor, you know that this person is methodical and relies on facts rather than feeling when making decisions. To relate to the inquisitor, you can use this information to incorporate data into your conversation rather than relying on intuition and emotion. The person to whom you have adapted will appreciate your insight and understanding.

Find common ground with the other person

Common ground is often considered small talk in interactions with other people. This part of communication is meant to break down barriers and find a topic to which all people involved can relate. Examples of common ground include mutual friends, shared interests, current events, or job-related topics.

Focus on mutually beneficial goals

To establish rapport, you must identify mutually beneficial goals early in the conversation. For example, in a meeting to resolve a conflict regarding office space, it benefits all parties involved to recognize that an efficient arrangement of workstations is the mutual goal. By focusing on that point, differing opinions might be expressed, but the rapport will continue because the parties are working toward a common goal.

Do it!

B-1:   Building rapport

Group discussions

1 In the following scene, Nicholas (supervisor) and John (subordinate) are seated at the table in Nicholas's office. There are day planners and folders on the table.

Nicholas: John, I hear we have a common golf buddy, Bill Brown.

John: You know Bill? He's a great guy. We've had some great times out on the golf course.

Nicholas: Oh, I bet. Bill's quite a character.

John: Well, any friend of Bill's is a friend of mine.

Nicholas: John, I'm glad our department heads set this meeting up. I think this is going to be a very successful partnership.

How is the rapport built in the given scenario?

2 In the following scene, Phyllis (supervisor), Julia (subordinate), and Matt (subordinate) are seated at the table in Phyllis's office. There are day planners and folders on the table.

Phyllis: Before we get started, let's identify our goals here today.

Julia: My goal is to keep Matt from stealing the best accounts from my salespeople!

Matt: And my goal is to make sure my salespeople get a fair number of active accounts, instead of the inactive accounts we're working with now.

Phyllis: Okay, you two. Hold on a second. Would it be fair to say that we all share the same goal—to disperse the accounts fairly and make sure that everybody has a similar percentage of viable accounts?

Julia: Yes. I'm sorry for getting angry. That's really what I'm looking for. I don't mind sharing some of our active accounts with Matt's team, but several accounts have had the same rep for years—there's a partnership there. I don't want to lose the relationships that we've built.

Matt: I understand that. But let's remember our goal—to give us both the same percentage of viable accounts. Maybe my team should get a larger share of the new accounts, since those relationships haven't been established yet.

Phyllis: That sounds fair. What do you think, Julia?

Julia: That could work. Let's start working on the numbers.

> Was Phyllis able to identify a common goal for Matt and Julia?
>
> How does identifying a common goal help?

Credibility

Explanation

Credibility is respect for and belief in a speaker. A speaker must have credibility to ensure that his or her message is understood correctly. If the speaker does not have credibility, the listener is not likely to pay attention to her. Even if the message is heard, it will be affected by the listener's distrust for the speaker, and the message will be distorted.

At the beginning of a conversation, the speaker has a clean slate. As the speaker begins to communicate, the listener begins to form opinions about the speaker's credibility. To establish credibility, you should follow these guidelines:

- Demonstrate competence.
- Build trust.
- Recognize similarities between speaker and listener.
- Exhibit sincerity.

Demonstrate competence

Listeners like to know that a speaker is knowledgeable about the topic. However, listeners don't like a braggart. Citing statistics and examples will lend competence to your words. In addition, being well prepared and well organized will help you demonstrate your competence as a speaker.

Build trust

Speakers often tell the truth in a conversation only to discover later that their listener did not believe what they said. If a listener has ever been lied to by a speaker, or has reason to believe that the speaker lied to others, he will distrust the speaker. It is important to speak honestly in every conversation to build a reputation for honesty.

Recognize similarities between speaker and listener

Frequently, listeners are apt to accept a speaker's opinions or ideas if they believe they have something in common with the speaker. By establishing common ground, the speaker displays similarities between herself and the listener. Attire and language can also lead listeners to feel a connection to a speaker.

Exhibit sincerity

Speakers commonly use compliments to gain the approval of their listeners. When a speaker offers positive and enthusiastic praise, listeners are likely to believe the speaker is sincere. Conversely, when a speaker uses negative expressions and lacks enthusiasm, she leaves listeners with a negative impression. Her compliments will become suspect, and her credibility will be in question.

Do it!

B-2: Establishing credibility

Exercise

1 One student will speak about "sharks" for two minutes and another student will speak about "cars" for two minutes.

How well did the student speaking about "sharks" demonstrate competence?

Was he or she able to build trust? Why?

How well did the student speaking about "cars" demonstrate competence?

Was he or she able to build trust? Why?

Topic C: Building positive relationships

Explanation

Often, it is necessary for the speaker to become the listener. Speakers occasionally need to request additional information to better communicate with their listeners. When a speaker asks a question, it gets the listener more involved with the conversation, which provides a circle of communication and encourages rapport.

Guidelines for asking questions

In order for a question to help build positive relationships, it must be clearly stated. Use these three guidelines to clarify your questions:

- Use unequivocal language.
- Use specific phrases.
- Avoid jargon.

Use unequivocal language

Unequivocal language leaves no room for questions and should be used whenever possible. Unequivocal terms have only one correct dictionary definition, so there is no room for misunderstanding. For example, you might ask a listener if a particular package arrived in Gainesville. Because you have not specified if the package to which you are referring was sent to Gainesville, Texas, or Gainesville, Florida, your listener might not be able to answer correctly. If you were to use unequivocal language, the listener would clearly understand what you were asking and would be able to answer with an equally direct response.

Use specific phrases

Often, two people become involved in a question-and-answer session when determining something that could have been said in one or two sentences. Using specific phrases saves time and money. If a co-worker tells you to "bring copies of the report to the meeting," you might need to ask several questions to determine the topic of the report, the time of the meeting, how many copies, and which specific meeting. If your co-worker had said, "Bring 20 copies of last quarter's sales report to the two o'clock meeting," the conversation would have been much more efficient.

Avoid jargon

Jargon is the vocabulary unique to a specific profession. Although it might expedite conversations in the workplace, jargon is ineffective if everyone does not understand the terminology. Be sure everyone involved in a conversation is familiar with the terms being used. If they are not, explain the meaning of any acronyms or other technical words or phrases.

Types of questions

Occasionally, you might find yourself asking questions even if they are not sincere requests for information. There are four types of insincere questions that you should avoid:

- Statement questions
- Hidden agenda questions
- Assumption questions
- Questions that seek a specific response

Statement questions

Statement questions are actually statements of fact or feeling disguised as questions. An example of a statement question is, "Do you think you should have turned in that report yesterday?" What the speaker is actually saying is, "You should have turned in that report yesterday." However, the speaker is being indirect and unclear in expressing her true feelings.

Hidden agenda questions

Hidden agenda questions mask the true intent of the speaker. You might be asked whether you have completed a certain task. The questioner is actually trying to ascertain whether you have time to help him with another task. Hidden agenda questions can be irritating and frustrating to the recipients once they answer the questions and discover that the speaker has a hidden agenda.

Assumption questions

Asking someone, "What's wrong?" assumes that something is the matter with that person. This question is an assumption question because the speaker assumes something to be a fact based on her perception. Keep in mind that perceptions are often misleading. Ask genuine, fact-finding questions to avoid making assumptions. For example, asking someone, "Why are you upset?" assumes that the person is upset, while asking "Are you upset?" seeks to determine the facts.

Questions that seek a specific response

Occasionally, a person asks a question hoping for a specific response. For example, if a boss asks an employee's opinion about a presentation or report, the boss might only be interested in hearing the "right" answer, which puts the employee in an uncomfortable situation. Be sure that any question you ask is sincere and that you are receptive to the person's honest opinion.

Do it!

C-1:   Asking questions

Exercises

1   Watch the movie clip and then answer the following questions.

What kind of question did Nicholas ask?

What assumption did Nicholas make?

What is the impact of asking questions based on a faulty assumption?

2   Identify the types of questions you should avoid asking.

A   Statement questions

B   Questions that seek a vague response

C   Determination questions

D   Questions that seek a specific response

E   False questions

F   Assumption questions

G   Hidden agenda questions

3 Your instructor will choose one student to play the role of a person who has just taken over as Interim Director of Industrial Casing Products. Senior management has assigned to the Interim Director the task of reducing the number of different styles of cases manufactured. This task is necessary to increase efficiency. The Interim Director now has to meet the managers of the marketing and engineering departments. This is his first interaction with them in his new role as their interim supervisor.

The Interim Director needs to make a positive first impression and build rapport while discussing changes to the industrial casing product line.

The Engineering Manager is a confident, sociable individual who is well liked in the company. He enjoys generating ideas and many employees seek his advice when confronted with a difficult problem. However, he dislikes managing the details involved in implementing his ideas and sometimes needs assistance to finish them.

The Marketing Manager is a quiet, intelligent individual who is dedicated and hard working. She prefers to work alone and is uncomfortable in group settings. She often will not share her ideas unless she is prompted or feels the conversation is severely off-track.

Was the Interim Director able to make a positive first impression?

What did he do to try to build rapport?

Do you think the Interim Director applied the guidelines for establishing credibility?

Unit summary: First impressions and building rapport

Topic A   In this unit, you learned about the **elements that influence a first impression**, including **appearance, knowledge, and social composure**.

Topic B   Then, you learned about the **guidelines** you should follow for **building rapport and credibility** with others. You learned how to establish rapport by **adapting to the other person's communication style, finding common ground, and focusing on mutually beneficial goals**. Then, you learned how to establish credibility by **demonstrating competency, building trust, and exhibiting sincerity**.

Topic C   Finally, you learned about the **guidelines for asking questions**, which include **using unequivocal language and specific phrases**, as well as **avoiding jargon**. You also learned about the **types of questions** you should avoid asking, such as **assumption questions, statement questions, hidden agenda questions and questions that seek a specific response**.

Independent practice activity

1 What elements influence first impressions?

2 What types of questions you should avoid asking?

3 Identify the question type of the following question: "Do you think you should have uploaded the sales report yesterday evening?"

   A Assumption

   B Generic

   C Statement

4 Identify the question type the following question: "Why were you upset during the meeting?"

   A Assumption

   B Generic

   C Statement

5 When demonstrating competence, citing statistics and examples lends credibility to the speaker's words.

   A True

   B False

Unit 3

Building relationships through feedback

Unit time: 45 minutes

Complete this unit, and you'll know how to:

A Use paraphrasing effectively.

B Provide positive and constructive feedback in a business setting.

Topic A: The importance of feedback

Explanation

Providing feedback for the speaker is an important element in building a relationship because it closes the circle of communication that links the listener and speaker. Until feedback is given, the people involved in communication are either speakers or listeners. However, once a speaker receives feedback, the roles switch and both parties are equally involved in a conversation.

Forms of feedback

As with other types of communication, feedback comes in two forms—verbal and nonverbal.

Verbal feedback

Verbal feedback is simply the words and phrases we use when responding to others. It might involve either a detailed answer to a question or a simple "yes" or "no." Most questions are a request for verbal feedback. For example, if you ask a co-worker to explain the process for filing a work order, you expect a clear, detailed response. Statements might or might not require verbal feedback. If you say that you do not understand how to file a work order, your co-worker might volunteer the information, or might simply not respond because you did not make a direct request. It is important to be clear about what type of verbal feedback you expect.

Nonverbal feedback

Whenever a listener receives a message, he or she always gives *nonverbal feedback*, whether in the form of a nod or shake of the head, a hand gesture, a questioning expression, or simply silence. This nonverbal feedback indicates the listener's thoughts and emotions about the speaker's original message.

Paraphrasing

Paraphrasing is the act of receiving a message, processing it, changing the language, and repeating it to ensure that you comprehend the intended message. Paraphrasing is important means of offering feedback because it ensures that the listener understood the message the speaker sent. The original speaker should respond to help the listener gauge her understanding of the message. Although paraphrasing might not always be done in a question form, its intent is to clarify and enhance understanding.

You can paraphrase the following three elements of a message:

- Topic
- Meaning
- Emotion

Topic

When you paraphrase the *topic* of a message, you simply change the words the speaker has used. For example, you might use synonyms in place of the original words and ask the original speaker if that is an accurate description of what he just said.

Meaning

Paraphrasing the *meaning* goes beyond the surface of the speaker's message. Instead of changing the words a speaker has used, you need to analyze the message's intent to determine its meaning. You then repeat the message in different words as a check. This paraphrasing technique is helpful when a speaker sends a message that could be interpreted in more than one way.

Emotion

Often, words do not fully tell the story behind the speaker's emotions. By listening and paraphrasing the feeling behind a statement, you are better able to comprehend it.

Imagine that a co-worker tells you, "I don't think Amy should have been promoted. She won't do a very good job." Is your co-worker expressing a lack of faith in Amy's abilities? Or is he disappointed and angry about being passed over for the promotion? Knowing the reason for a message gives the listener a better idea of what the speaker is trying to express.

Do it!

A-1:   Using paraphrasing

Group discussions

1 Watch the movie clip and then answer the following questions.

What is being paraphrased in the given discussion?

How did paraphrasing help?

2 In the following scene, Carlene (supervisor) and Brett (subordinate) are seated at the table in the conference room. There are day planners and folders on the table.

Brett: I wish that Research and Development would hurry up with the annual report. We've been waiting on it for weeks! I can't believe they're so slow. They're always running behind.

Carlene: It sounds like you have an important reason for wanting that report. Is your annual sales forecast coming due?

Brett: Yes. I can't plug in the numbers until I get them from R and D.

What did element Carlene paraphrase in the discussion?

Were Brett's comments ambiguous?

3 In the following scene, Phyllis (supervisor) and Nicholas (supervisor) are seated at the table in the conference room. There are day planners and folders on the table.

Phyllis: Nicholas, I heard that you had some concerns about the new schedule.

Nicholas: Yes. From what I understand, everybody's schedule will change. I just don't think that's fair. We're so used to our current schedules, and now we have to adjust our lives to a new one. It's going to be a big mess.

Phyllis: Well, Nicholas, you sound really worried. Let me see if I can eliminate some of your anxiety. Everybody's schedule might change, but some people will still be on the current schedule. It sounds like you might have a reason to keep your schedule the same. If that's the case, let me know, and we'll make sure you're on that list.

Nicholas: Really? That would be great. I'm really concerned that I won't be able to pick up my daughter from daycare on time, but if I can keep the same schedule, it would really be a big help.

Phyllis: Sure. Nicholas, don't ever be afraid to come to me with concerns. We'll work them out as best we can.

What element did Phyllis paraphrase?

Was Phyllis able to see the emotion and feeling behind Nicholas's statement?

Topic B: Providing feedback

Explanation

Positive feedback reinforces positive behavior. Following a process for providing such feedback enables you to be more effective because you'll provide the recipient with specific, detailed information. Sometimes, however, you need to provide employees with feedback on how to improve their behavior. By following a process for delivering constructive criticism, you can effectively encourage employees to change detrimental behaviors.

The process for providing positive feedback

The process for providing positive feedback consists of four steps:

1 Describe the positive behavior.
2 Explain why the behavior is positive.
3 Help the individual accept credit.
4 Thank and encourage the individual.

Describe the positive behavior

Accurately describe the individual's behavior in as much detail as possible. The more descriptive you are in your feedback, the better the recipient will understand and recognize her positive behavior. The desired result of positive feedback is to encourage the recipient to repeat the positive behavior. However, to do so, she must be able to recognize such behavior. When providing feedback, be sure to describe where and when the behavior took place, as well as what was specifically desirable about it.

Explain why the behavior is positive

Helping an individual understand the reason that her behavior was positive is critical to demonstrating how she fits into the big picture. Someone who sees herself as a contributor to the department or organization is more likely to be motivated in the future.

Help the individual accept credit

Sometimes, employees try to shrug off praise or compliments. It is important that you help employees understand their contribution and accept the positive feedback. Start by providing specific examples of the positive behavior they have displayed. Next, help employees realize the importance of their actions by showing them how their behavior has benefited the team, department, or company.

Thank and encourage the individual

The final step for providing positive feedback is to express your appreciation by thanking the individual for her efforts. Doing so helps her feel more self-confident and satisfied with her work. When you thank an employee, you should also encourage her to continue the desired behavior.

Do it!

B-1:   Providing positive feedback

Exercises

1   Put the steps for providing positive feedback in proper order, eliminating any unnecessary steps.

Help the individual accept credit

Consult human resources for permission to praise the employee

Thank and encourage the individual

Explain why the behavior is positive

Describe the positive behavior

Explain the negative behavior

2   Read the following scene and then identify where the different steps for providing feedback are used.

John: Well Laura! Let me compliment you in achieving your targets and generating high morale among your team members.

Laura: Thanks John. However, most of the credit goes to my team. They've done all the hard work.

John: It's true that you team has done a good job, but only because of your guidance. You have shown us a different path by which productivity can be increased while keeping stress levels low. In the past, we've lost a number of valuable employees who left because of high stress, which is why we really appreciate your work. You sincerely deserve this credit.

Laura: Thank you sir.

John: Thank you very much for this excellent year. We look forward to a similar performance from you next year.

Laura: I'll do my best.

Providing constructive feedback

Explanation

When given properly, constructive feedback encourages employees to change negative behaviors for the better. However, when done improperly, such feedback can discourage employees, making them feel frustrated. The purpose of constructive feedback is to improve the recipient's job performance, so it is important to provide prompt and accurate guidance.

The process for giving individuals constructive feedback consists of the following five steps:

1 Identify the problem behavior.
2 Explain how the behavior is detrimental.
3 Help the individual acknowledge the problem.
4 Develop goals with the individual.
5 Monitor the individual's performance.

Identify the problem behavior

Begin a constructive feedback session by informing the individual that you have become aware of the problem behavior, and use specific examples to describe the behavior. Discuss where and when the behavior took place. The more accurate and detailed your description, the easier it will be for the recipient to understand what he needs to change. Focus on the person's actions and behaviors that are the cause for the feedback instead of focusing on his personality or attributes. This technique will help prevent the recipient from feeling as though he is being personally attacked.

Explain how the behavior is detrimental

After you've explained the negative behaviors, help the individual understand how the behavior is detrimental. By explaining how the behavior impacts other people and the organization, the recipient can understand how his actions affect productivity. When a recipient understands the effects of his actions, he is usually willing to make the necessary changes in behavior.

Help the individual acknowledge the problem

Occasionally, an individual resists acknowledging some or all of the problems his behavior causes. If this occurs, you need to give specific examples that show the effects of the recipient's negative behavior.

Once you have provided sufficient evidence to show the impact of an individual's actions, he usually agrees that a problem exists and is willing to make an effort to change the behavior. However, if the individual refuses to acknowledge the problem, or does not change his behavior, you might need to explain to him that he might face negative consequences for his actions. Describing consequences can help the individual understand the severity of the problem.

Develop goals with the individual

After the individual has agreed that he needs to modify his behavior, you should work with him to develop goals. A behavioral goal needs to be specific, obtainable, and measurable. Determine a specific time frame in which the changes should occur, and thoroughly describe how the changes will happen. It is important to involve the individual in setting behavioral goals so that he feels a sense of ownership and dedication to the goals.

Monitor the individual's performance

Monitoring the individual's performance will improve the chances of his successfully changing his behavior. Once you and the individual have agreed upon goals, set up a system to monitor his performance. One way to monitor progress is to plan regular meetings with the individual. Such meetings provide an opportunity to measure his progress toward the agreed-upon goals.

Do it!

B-2: Providing constructive feedback

Exercises

1 Put the steps for providing constructive feedback in proper order, eliminating any unnecessary steps.

Thank and encourage the individual

Develop goals with the individual

Explain how the behavior is detrimental

Describe the positive behavior

Identify the problem behavior

Monitor the individual's performance

Help the individual acknowledge the problem

2 Read the following scene.

John: Well Thomas, how has the quarter been?

Thomas: We exceeded our targets and are doing very well.

John: What about the cost to the company as a result of the increased turnover or personnel?

Thomas: Well! That's HR's concern, not mine.

John: Do you know that your abrasive methods have taken a huge toll and we are having problems getting the right people? Experienced people are also leaving.

Thomas: I think better salaries can take care of that.

John: Why are you so rude Thomas?

Thomas: I'm not rude, John. If you think I am, maybe I should start giving flowers to people and shaking hands every morning.

John: Do you really understand what I am trying to say?

Thomas: Do you understand me or even try to?

John: This is not leading anywhere. I want to meet with you again tomorrow.

Thomas: I'm traveling and meeting customers for the next seven days. Can we meet eight days from now?

John: Okay. I think something is wrong somewhere.

Why do you think this meeting went bad?

From where exactly did the discussion go off track?

What kind of response from whom could have gotten the situation under control?

3   Your instructor will choose one student to play the role of a person who has just taken over as Interim Director of Industrial Casing Products. This person has to meet with the Production Manager for casing products, who is responsible for the actual manufacturing of the industrial casing product line. The production rate and the employee morale are high for this manager's team. However, there have been problems with the quality of cases produced. Almost 10-percent are scrapped because of defects.

The Interim Director has to provide the Production Manager with both positive and constructive feedback.

The Production Manager is a hard working employee who started as a production employee and worked up to the position of a production manager. Because of past achievements, the Production Manager is admired by his employer and is often asked to be a peacemaker between management and the production group. While often deferential to others when confronted with difficult decisions, this manager is not afraid to take a stand if he or she feels an idea or plan is not practical or affects production employees in a negative way.

Was the Interim Director able to provide positive and constructive feedback?

Did everything go well during the discussion?

What could have been better?

Unit summary: Building relationships through feedback

Topic A

In this unit, you learned about **verbal** and **nonverbal** forms of feedback. You also learned to **use paraphrasing effectively** to ensure that you understand the meaning behind a speaker's statements.

Topic B

Finally, you learned how to provide **positive feedback** by **recognizing the positive behavior, describing why it was positive, helping the individual accept credit, and thanking the person**. You also learned to provide **constructive feedback** in a business setting by **identifying the problem behavior, explaining why it is detrimental, helping the employee acknowledge the problem, developing goals, and monitoring the employee's performance**.

Independent practice activity

1   How do you paraphrase a speaker's statements?

2   When giving constructive feedback to your subordinate, you explained to him how his or her behavior was detrimental. What should you do next?

   A   Monitor his or her performance

   B   Identify the problem behavior

   C   Develop goals with the subordinate

   D   Help the individual acknowledge the problem

3   Positive feedback encourages an individual to change his or her negative behavior.

   A   True

   B   False

4   Why should you thank people for their efforts?

5   Paraphrasing the _____ goes beyond the surface of the speaker's message.

   A   Meaning

   B   Topic

   C   Emotion

Unit 4

Supervisors

Unit time: 45 minutes

Complete this unit, and you'll know how to:

A Identify the types of ineffective supervisors and interact with an ineffective supervisor, promote an idea, and accept constructive criticism.

B Negotiate a raise with a supervisor and offer an effective resignation.

Topic A: Understanding supervisor styles

Explanation

When you think of a supervisor, you probably think of your immediate boss. However, in the workplace, most people have several supervisors. Your workplace might be divided into teams, departments or divisions. Within each level, there is a supervisor to whom you are accountable, even if you do not deal with that person on a day-to-day basis. Company executives and board members can also be considered supervisors because they might have the power to make decisions regarding your employment, salary, promotions, and work assignments. It is important to communicate effectively with all of your supervisors to maintain an efficient workplace and to be able to promote your own ideas for improvements.

Qualities of an effective supervisor

Effective supervisors share an important quality—the desire to serve their employees. Competent supervisors realize that it is their job to keep things operating smoothly in the workplace. To ensure this occurs, they listen to suggestions and follow through when possible. Communicating with this type of supervisor is usually easy because such supervisors maintain an open-door policy.

Types of ineffective supervisors

Unfortunately, many supervisors allow some particular aspect of their personalities to affect their interactions with employees, which hinders effective communication. The following are five types of ineffective supervisors:

- Bully
- Guilt tripper
- Blamer
- Dreamer
- Emotional volcano

Bully

Bullies bask in their own authority. They will most likely use body language to suggest superiority, such as crossed arms and peering over eyeglasses. Threats are a key component of the bully's communication style. A bully often uses phrases such as, "You'd better get that done" or "I need this done right now."

To communicate with the bully, it is important to remind yourself that this person is human and should not be regarded fearfully. Also, find a way to compliment the bully. By complimenting your supervisor, you'll feel more powerful and less intimidated when the supervisor tries to bully you.

Guilt tripper

Supervisors who use guilt trips to motivate employees are using a passive-aggressive style of supervising. For example, they might say that they do not mind staying late while everyone else goes home, but their body language tells a different story. Rather than asking directly for help, the *guilt tripper* will attempt to earn pity to get a specific response, such as getting an employee to stay late to work on a special project.

When dealing with guilt trippers, first establish what they are asking you to do. Determine if the task is as pressing as the guilt tripper would like you to believe. If she is being unreasonable, and you have a legitimate excuse for not immediately working on the guilt tripper's task, use it. However, the best way to communicate with a guilt tripper is to make definite plans to help her at a time that is convenient for both of you. By doing so, both you and the guilt tripper will feel satisfied that the job is going to get done in a timely fashion, and you'll have responded in a way that demonstrates a team effort.

Blamer

Some supervisors respond with blame when errors are discovered. Should you encounter a *blamer*, it is important to focus on the facts of the situation. Your goal is not to establish fault, but to understand what can be done to remedy the situation. Be willing to accept responsibility for the situation. However, accepting responsibility is not the same thing as accepting blame. Accepting responsibility conveys an attitude of willingness to resolve the situation without focusing on who is at fault. Above all, remain calm. Do not feed into the anger or anxiety of the blamer.

Dreamer

At some point in your career, you might encounter a supervisor who is a *dreamer*. This supervisor not only has many ideas, but also has complete confidence in himself. The dreamer is likely to come up with a new idea every week and expects full support from his employees. Communicating with a dreamer can be tricky because you do not want to neglect an idea that might be profitable for your company; however, it would be too time consuming and inefficient to act on each of the dreamer's suggestions. When the dreamer presents a new idea to you, first determine the logistics of the situation. Determine what priority your supervisor wants to give this project. Then, give yourself some time to review it in private. Make a list of questions to ask your supervisor about the idea's feasibility. For example, you might ask your supervisor to explain cost projections, marketability, or industry impact. While it should not be your intention to shoot down new ideas, you need to make sure that each idea is workable before it becomes your project and your potential failure.

Emotional volcano

The *emotional volcano* reacts to fear and frustration through yelling, ranting, and fist pounding. This supervisor thinks that she can motivate employees through fear. Unfortunately, this behavior often motivates employees to look for a new job.

If you find yourself dealing with an emotional volcano, try to identify what is motivating her to react in an emotional way. For example, an emotional volcano who is worried about her own upcoming performance review might get angry during your performance review. Understanding the cause of the supervisor's emotions will help you communicate with her because you'll realize that you are not the true target of her emotions.

Another important point to keep in mind when communicating with an emotional volcano is to avoid telling her to calm down. Nobody likes to be told what emotions to feel, so telling someone to calm down is more likely to increase her rage than not. You should set an example by remaining calm. Use language that promotes a team effort to work through the situation. Above all, never let yourself get involved in a shouting match.

Do it!

A-1: Handling ineffective supervisors

Exercises

1 Watch the movie clip and then answer the following questions.

What type of boss is Patricia?

Was Laurie able to handle Patricia?

Which statement in the discussion set the interaction right?

2 Watch the movie clip and then answer the following questions.

What kind of boss is Carlene?

Was Pam able to handle the situation?

Which statement in the given discussion set the interaction right?

3 In the following scene, Benjamin (supervisor) and John (subordinate) are seated at the table in Benjamin's office.

Benjamin: You completely screwed up this order!

John: Benjamin, I don't understand what went wrong. Tell me exactly what's wrong about it.

Benjamin: We're supposed to ship out the Centurion 2000, but the customer received the 3000 instead. You must've written the wrong number down, and now I've got an angry customer who got the wrong item.

John: Benjamin, I'd be happy to take care of that. Let me call the warehouse and arrange for the 2000 to be delivered. They can pick up the 3000 at the same time. I'll also arrange for the customer to receive a gift certificate to make up for the error.

Benjamin: Okay. That should keep the customer happy.

What is Benjamin trying to do?

What did John do to accept
responsibility for solving the
problem?

4 In the following scene, John (subordinate) and Julia (subordinate) are seated at the table in John's office.

John: What are you working on?

Julia: Ms. Bannon had yet another idea for the new Centurion. Actually, this one sounds like it might be workable, but I'm making a list of questions to ask her to see if she's really thought this through. I don't want to go ahead with a plan that hasn't been studied carefully.

John: What kinds of things do you plan to ask her?

Julia: Well, cost is always the biggest issue. I want to hear her plan for keeping costs down because this idea involves using a more expensive plastic than we've used in the past. I just want to determine the amount of research that's gone into this idea.

What kind of boss is Ms. Bannon?

What did Julia do in the given
situation?

5   Read the following scene. In the scene, Phyllis (supervisor) and Matt (subordinate) are seated in Phyllis's office.

Phyllis: And that is why I have to have those numbers on my desk by Wednesday morning!

Matt: Ms. Bannon, I understand that the company is counting on the sales department to furnish the projections for next Thursday's meeting. If we don't have the numbers, it will reflect badly on all of us. I know we can work together to get it done. Can we set aside Monday afternoon to finalize the report?

Phyllis: Yes, I think I can clear my schedule. Let's get the whole department together Monday. If we can get that report done early, it would be a huge relief.

What do you is think is happening in this situation?

What did Matt do to complete the sales projection?

6   Match each set of characteristics to one of the following types of ineffective supervisor: bully, dreamer, blamer, emotional volcano, or guilt tripper.

Uses threats to motivate

Continually offers new ideas

Tries to place blame on employee

Yelling, ranting, fist pounding

Says one thing and means another

7   In the table below, identify your supervisors, their type, and the type of relationship you have with them.

Name	Role	Department	Type of relationship (good/bad)

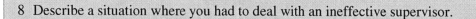

8 Describe a situation where you had to deal with an ineffective supervisor.

9 How could you have changed your style of communication to make a more favorable impression on the supervisor?

Promoting ideas

Explanation

Preparation is the key to successfully promoting an idea to a supervisor. Your presentation might involve a conversation in your supervisor's office or a company meeting with handouts, charts, and a slide show. Regardless of the situation, you can follow these guidelines to ensure a quality presentation:

- Become the expert.
- Prepare your materials.
- Take ownership of your idea.

Become the expert

Do as much research as possible to become an expert about your topic. You'll also find it helpful to discuss the proposal with co-workers before your meeting to find out if any issues are unclear to them. This preparation will enable you to anticipate any questions that might arise during your presentation.

Prepare materials

If the presentation of your idea is going to be in an informal setting, you'll probably have few materials to prepare, if any. However, if your presentation is going to be in front of a team or board, you might want to prepare handouts for each person who will be present. Handouts will give your audience a reference to your idea once the meeting is over. If you'll be using equipment, such as a laptop or slide projector, give yourself plenty of time before the meeting to set up the equipment and be sure that everything is working properly. Also, always have a backup plan in case your equipment fails. For example, if you've prepared a chart on a laptop that shows your proposed restructuring of the sales department, bring along a paper version in case your technology fails. If your technology is not working properly, you might lose credibility with your supervisor and she might not give your idea the attention it deserves.

Take ownership of your idea

You do not want to present an idea to your supervisor only to have the project turned over to another employee. From the beginning of your presentation, use "I" and "we" when speaking about the future of your idea to indicate your interest in following through with the idea. This type of positive language will also communicate a desire to work in cooperation with your supervisor. If necessary, include in your presentation a description of how you'll rearrange your current responsibilities to facilitate your new idea.

Handling feedback

Although modesty is a desirable trait, it is often makes it difficult for employees to accept a compliment from their supervisors. If you find yourself on the receiving end of positive feedback, begin your acceptance with a simple "thank you." Express your regard for your supervisor and explain why the compliment is important to you. If anybody should share in the positive feedback, be sure to tell your supervisor so that your colleagues can be recognized.

Unfortunately, not all feedback from your supervisor will necessarily be positive. If you are the recipient of constructive feedback, take the opportunity to learn from the situation. Ask your supervisor which areas you can work on to improve your performance. Listen to everything your supervisor has to say rather than acting defensively or trying to shift the blame to others. If you feel that the criticism is unjust, try to understand how your supervisor has perceived the situation. Keep in mind that perception varies from person to person. Perhaps your performance has been outstanding but your supervisor has not been made aware of your achievements. If you cannot find anything to change about your performance, make an effort to open the lines of communication with your supervisor and be your own cheerleader. Your supervisor cannot reward you for a superior effort if he or she is unaware of your accomplishments.

Do it!

A-2: Promoting an idea

Multiple-choice question

1 Which guidelines should you follow when promoting an idea to your supervisor?

 A Let supervisor direct meeting

 B Prepare your materials

 C Take ownership of your idea

 D Become the expert

 E Use specific language

Topic B: Handling human resource issues

Explanation

Negotiating for a raise or tendering your resignation are among some of the most delicate issues you have to deal with as an employee. Both situations require you to use tact and discretion, but to nonetheless express your ideas and desires clearly.

Negotiating for a raise

Although it is easy to list reasons why you need or want a raise, it is not guaranteed that your supervisor will take a personal interest in those reasons. The only sure way to persuade your supervisor that you deserve a raise is by demonstrating superior performance on the job.

The following steps will help you present a positive impression on your supervisor when you ask for a raise:

1   Focus on how you meet and exceed the demands of your job.
2   Highlight your accomplishments.
3   Research salaries and company history.
4   Mentally review and prepare for your presentation.
5   Dress for the part.
6   Make a good impression.

Focus on how you meet and exceed the demands of your job

Although eloquent language will help you communicate effectively when negotiating a raise, it is facts and figures that will determine your supervisor's receptiveness to your proposal. Before your meeting, look at your job description to be sure that you are exceeding the minimum requirements for your position. Find data to support your case. For example, if your job description states that you are to successfully maintain 20 accounts per year, and you are successfully maintaining 25 accounts, you are exceeding your job requirements. You should share this fact during your salary negotiation.

Highlight your accomplishments

If you were employee of the month or helped your department earn a bonus for quarterly sales figures, be sure to highlight those accomplishments during salary negotiations. However, make sure your accomplishments are related to the company. For example, suppose you coordinated a team from your department to compete in a charity fundraiser that provided free advertising to corporate participants. You should include that information because it shows how you positively affected the organization.

Research salaries and company history

Before asking your supervisor for a salary increase, have a clear understanding of how your current salary compares to the industry standard. Gather information on salaries for similar positions within similar companies, and use this information to formulate a target salary. If the average is significantly higher than your current wage, include that information in your negotiations. If you are already earning more than the industry average, consider offering to take on further responsibilities in exchange for an increased salary.

You should also research your own company's history. Start by reading your company's annual report. The previous year's earnings will most likely give you an indication of whether your supervisor will even have the ability to grant you a raise. This information can also suggest if it might be prudent to request additional responsibilities in addition to your raise.

Mentally review and prepare for your presentation

Although you do not want to sound like you are reading from a script during your salary negotiation, you do want your presentation to flow smoothly. Make a mental note of the key elements you want to include in your request, such as job requirements, accomplishments, and salary information. You should prepare a format that allows your request to sound natural and comfortable. Then, think of potential arguments to your request and prepare counter-arguments. After mentally preparing for your presentation, you should set up an appointment with your supervisor. It is best to plan this meeting for a part of the day when things are relatively calm. Do not set a salary negotiation for Monday morning or Friday afternoon, and do not set your meeting for first thing in the morning or immediately prior to closing time, as these are the usually most hectic times of the day. If your supervisor is distracted by weekend plans or by the tasks of beginning or ending the day, he is less likely to give you his full attention, and your salary request might not be taken seriously.

Dress for the part

Your attire is an important element of communication because others form impressions based on your clothing. The way you dress can affect others' perceptions of you and your message. It is important to dress appropriately for a salary negotiation to demonstrate competence and confidence in yourself. Although this meeting is an important event, do not drastically change your wardrobe. Wear normal business attire, but take extra care to ensure that your outfit is freshly laundered and pressed.

Make a good impression

As you enter the meeting room for your salary negotiation, be polite and courteous without being overly formal. For example, if first names are commonly used between your supervisor and his or her employees, do not use a formal title such as Mr. or Mrs. for this meeting. Using a formal title when inappropriate will make your delivery seem stilted and create an uncomfortable atmosphere. Begin the meeting by thanking your supervisor for agreeing to meet with you. Being polite and courteous will demonstrate respect for your supervisor and will encourage her to listen to your request. Make strong eye contact with your supervisor and try to sit in a position similar to hers. If possible, eliminate any obstacles, such as desks, that stand between you and your supervisor. If such a seating arrangement is not possible, then sit as close to the desk as possible. Eliminating or minimizing obstacles will create an atmosphere of cooperation. If you have practiced delivering the key points of your salary request, your presentation should flow comfortably and naturally.

Do it!

B-1:   Negotiating a raise

1 Why do you think it is important to research the comparable salaries for your position before negotiating for a raise?

2 The Quality Control Manager in the Plastic Casing Department has to meet with his or her supervisor to negotiate a raise. It has been two years since the manager received a pay increase. This manager is a hardworking leader with a positive attitude.

The last year of the Quality Control Manager's career has been very successful. The manager served on a variety of departmental teams and committees where the manager's inputs were highly regarded. The Quality Control Manager was named manager of the month twice and received the prestigious Icon Horizon Award for a study he or she headed up. This study resulted in the development of a process for shaping plastics that will save both time and money over $85,000 per year. Finally, the manager also coordinated a campaign to raise public awareness of Icon's Environmental Protection Measures, which helped bring in several large clients.

In preparation of this meeting, this manager analyzed what other Quality Control Managers in similar companies are paid, and discovered that the salary he or she receives is slightly less than the industry norm. The manager also reviewed the job description and knows that his or her involvement in the Extrusion Efficiency Study far exceeds the minimum requirements of the job.

The supervisor is the Production Manager for the Plastic Casing Department of Icon's International Services and Manufacturing Division. This supervisor is a tough but fair manager, and is notorious for taking hard-line approach to employees' work ethics. The supervisor demands outstanding performances from them. This supervisor rewards his employees for good service, but does so only when convinced beyond a doubt that the reward is deserved. The supervisor can be pushy and overbearing at times, and is easily agitated.

What kind of boss is the Production Manager?

Was the Quality Control Manager able to negotiate the raise?

What went wrong during the discussion?

Resigning from your job

Explanation

In the workplace, resignations need to be handled delicately. Although your immediate goal is to terminate your employment, you might also want to keep the lines of communication open for possible counteroffers or future consideration. When submitting a resignation, you should follow these four guidelines:

- Be as detailed as possible.
- Use positive language.
- Do not burn bridges.
- Offer to aid in a smooth transition.

Be as detailed as possible

Communicate to your supervisor that you have received another offer or made the decision to leave the company. Explain the details, including salary, benefits, and anything else that makes the offer attractive. This information will help your supervisor form a counteroffer, if she chooses to do so.

Use positive language

Regardless of the situation you are leaving, make the meeting as upbeat as possible. Thank your supervisor for the opportunities you had to learn and grow in your position. Keep your language positive by focusing on what the other company has done to attract you, rather than on the negative aspects you'll be leaving behind.

Do not burn bridges

Even if you have decided not to accept any counteroffers, be sure to leave the door open to that possibility. A counteroffer could be more attractive than the new position. Also, situations change, and you might find yourself once again seeking a position with your old company. Make a commitment to keep the lines of communication open at your previous workplace.

Offer to aid in a smooth transition

One of your supervisor's fears might be finding a suitable replacement. Offer to stay with the company throughout the hiring process so that you can train the new hire. If staying throughout this process is not possible, prepare or revise training documents for your position to assist in a seamless transition between yourself and the new employee.

Do it!

B-2: Resigning from a job

1 What are the four steps you should follow when resigning from a job?

2 Why should you prepare training documents for your position?

Unit summary: Supervisors

Topic A   In this unit, you learned how to **identify** and **interact with different types of ineffective supervisors**, including bullies, guilt trippers, blamers, dreamers, and emotional volcano. You also learned **how to promote an idea** and how **to deal with constructive criticism from a subordinate**.

Topic B   Finally, you learned about the steps for **negotiating a raise** and for **resigning from a job**.

Independent practice activity

1 What three steps should you follow when promoting an idea to a supervisor?

2 Which of the following supervisor uses threats to motivate his or her subordinates?

   A Bully

   B Dreamer

   C Blamer

   D Guilt tripper

3 Which of the following supervisors says one thing and means another?

   A Bully

   B Dreamer

   C Emotional volcano

   D Guilt tripper

4 What should you do before asking your supervisor for a salary increase?

5 A supervisor who uses guilt trips to motivate employees uses an active, aggressive style of supervising.

   A True

   B False

Unit 5

Colleagues and subordinates

Unit time: 30 minutes

Complete this unit, and you'll know how to:

A Identify the guidelines for communicating with colleagues.

B Take appropriate steps to apologize to subordinates, use appropriate tactics to refuse a subordinate's request, and dismiss a subordinate.

Topic A: Communicating with colleagues

Explanation

Colleagues might include people in your office, team, department, or division. They do not hold a supervisory position over you, nor do you hold a supervisory position over them. Instead, you are all in a similar place on the corporate ladder. Learning how to communicate effectively with your colleagues helps maintain a friendly and effective workplace and enables you to better promote your ideas and respond to those of others.

Guidelines for communicating with colleagues

There are a few guidelines to remember when communicating with your colleagues:

- Demonstrate respect.
- Establish ground rules and responsibilities.
- Be honest about your thoughts and feelings.

Demonstrate respect

There are many ways in which you can show respect for your colleagues. Often, it is the everyday actions that make the greatest impact on your colleagues, such as listening and showing interest in a conversation. However, you can show respect in other ways as well. For example, if a colleague has helped you with a project for which you have received a reward, be sure that your supervisor knows that your colleague is also deserves recognition.

Establish ground rules and responsibilities

Colleagues can often become territorial about job responsibilities and physical space in the workplace. The easiest way to minimize these frustrations is to openly communicate and set ground rules that everyone can respect. By eliminating issues such as boundaries and job responsibilities, you can improve communication between colleagues.

Be honest about your thoughts and feelings

If you have a problem with a colleague, it cannot be remedied until that colleague is made aware of the situation. Be open and honest if there is a problem, so it can be solved quickly. Also, share positive thoughts and feelings to communicate a spirit of teamwork within your organization.

Promoting ideas among colleagues

To effectively promote an idea to your colleagues, you must envision yourself as the idea's champion. The champion of an idea is the person who is willing to fight for an idea and see it through to the finish. This person must recruit colleagues who are willing to invest their support in a project. When seeking your colleagues' support, carefully choose your allies. It is important that each colleague feels a sense of ownership over the project or idea, so keep your group small. Talk to your colleagues individually and let them know that you truly value their opinions and support. Once you have their support, you are better prepared to promote the idea to management.

Responding to an idea

Whether you support or disagree with a colleague's idea, it is important to keep your feedback positive and specific. It is easy to keep the tone of positive feedback light. However, you can also keep constructive feedback upbeat by making suggestions for improvement. In addition, the more specific you make your comments, the more helpful they will be to your colleague. For example, telling your colleague that an idea is not cost effective is much more helpful than simply saying that an idea will not work.

Do it!

A-1: Responding to a colleague's idea

Exercises

1 Watch the movie clip and then answer the following questions.

How did John respond to Julia's idea?

What guidelines should you follow when responding to a colleague's idea?

2 Identify the guidelines for communicating with colleagues.

A   Be guarded in conversations

B   Be territorial

C   Bring gifts for colleagues

D   Be honest about your thoughts and feelings

E   Act indifferent

F   Demonstrate respect

G   Establish ground rules and responsibilities

3 Identify colleagues with whom you have a good or bad relationship.

Name	Role	Department	Type of relationship (good/bad)

4 List the names of colleagues with whom you do not interact much and why you do not interact with them.

5 What should you do to make interacting with these colleagues a positive experience?

Topic B: Communicating with subordinates

Explanation

A subordinate is anyone who might look to you for guidance, work assignments, salary increases, promotions, or other assistance in the workplace. To a subordinate, you are an authority figure. However, it is important to eliminate the power struggle between subordinates and supervisors. Keep in mind that subordinates have the same daily struggles both in and out of the workplace as you do, and that regardless of your role in the organization, you share the same goal—to promote an efficient, friendly, and cost-effective workplace. However, if you are in a supervisory position, you will often have to deal with delicate issues involving your subordinates, such as apologizing, refusing their requests, and even dismissing them. Effective communication skills can help you handle such situations tactfully and smoothly.

Apologizing to subordinates

Occasionally, a supervisor might make an error for which he needs to apologize to his subordinates. If you find yourself in this situation, you should follow these four steps:

1 Assess the error and the damage it has caused.
2 Offer a sincere apology.
3 Listen to those who have been affected by your error.
4 Propose and explain solutions.

Assess the error and the damage that has been caused

Before apologizing, do some research on the situation. Determine the cause of the error and what you could have done differently to prevent it from occurring. Note the effects of the error and what is being done to correct it. You will need to address these issues will in your apology.

Offer a sincere apology

Above all, your apology needs to be sincere. If you do not understand the effects of your actions, ask a supervisor to explain them to you. By understanding how you have affected your organization and your subordinates, you'll be able to demonstrate sincerity in your apology.

Listen to those who have been affected by your error

Ask your subordinates to share the effects they have seen and felt as a result of your error. Find out from your subordinates what you can do to ease the negative effects they might have suffered.

Propose and explain solutions

Should an error occur, your subordinates will likely be most concerned with finding a solution. Formulate and share several potential solutions with your subordinates, and consider their opinions when determining the most effective solution.

Responding to a subordinate's constructive feedback

Regardless of how well you manage, there will be times when your subordinates will have constructive feedback for you. Should you receive constructive feedback from a subordinate, stay calm and listen to everything that she has to say. Paraphrase the message to show that you have listened and understood your subordinate's concern. Ask your subordinate if she has suggestions to resolve the issue. Indicate your willingness to work with the subordinate to a mutually satisfying solution, and follow through on that intention.

Refusing a request

As a supervisor, you will occasionally find yourself in a situation where you have to refuse a subordinate's request. If this situation should arise, be gentle but clear with your answer. If there is a possibility that your answer might change in the future, let the subordinate know the information and the details of what could cause your answer to change. This information can help your subordinate prepare for a second proposal should the situation change. However, if there is no possibility of your answer changing, be clear when explaining this decision to avoid promoting false hope. Give your subordinates reasons why you have to refuse their requests, and if appropriate, offer alternative solutions. It is important to emphasize the positive aspects of a subordinate's request because you do not want to stifle communication between yourself and your subordinates.

Do it!

B-1: Refusing a subordinate's request

Exercises
1 Watch the movie clip and then answer the following questions.
Did Patricia offer Pam a clear answer?
How did Patricia create an environment for continued communication?
2 Examine the following actions and then put the steps for apologizing to your subordinates in the proper order.
Listen to those who have been affected by your error
Propose and explain solutions
Offer a sincere apology
Assess the error and the damage that has been caused

3 Pat Kramer has to meet two engineers in the Research and Development Department of Icon's Industrial Services and Manufacturing Division. These engineers are designing experimental equipment for the Plastic Casing department that will be more efficient. This equipment is called EE3. A few days after the engineers received the design specifications for EE3, senior management added a new stipulation to the specifications. The equipment must now be capable of dealing with a second composite material, MF-315, as well as the original material, MF-300. Pat was part of the meeting and knew about this apparently minor change. However, because of a miscommunication, the two engineers were not made aware of the change and their current designs accommodate only MF-300. Consequently, they must alter the designs. The deadline to complete their designs is one week away. This deadline is not negotiable.

Pat needs to find a solution to the problem. If Pat discovers that the miscommunication was due to an error on his/her part, Pat must effectively apologize to the engineers. It is probable that they will ask for more time to complete the designs. If so, Pat must effectively refuse their request.

The first engineer is an intelligent and systematic individual. This person's attention to detail and need for precision make the person an excellent engineer. However, these qualities can make the first engineer somewhat hard to work with because this person always wants things done right the first time. The first does not deal with change well, and has a short temper that often makes it communication difficult.

The second engineer is a hard working individual with an easy going attitude. This person is known for patience, determination, and good humor. The second engineer believes there is a way to work out every problem, and only becomes frustrated when the lines of communication break down and progress toward a solution ceases.

Do you think Pat created this situation?

Was Pat able to refuse the engineers' request for more time for completing the designs?

What went right during their discussion?

What went wrong during their discussion?

Dismissing a subordinate

Explanation

Occasionally, you'll need to dismiss a subordinate. The reasons might vary from behavioral issues to company layoffs, but whatever the reason, it can be a difficult situation for both supervisors and subordinates. There are five steps to follow when dismissing a subordinate:

1. Explain the reason for the dismissal.
2. Give the effective date of dismissal.
3. Provide details about the dismissal.
4. Offer positive measures that might be taken on the subordinate's behalf.
5. Provide an official written notice of dismissal.

Explain the reason for the dismissal

Clearly explain to the subordinate the situation that caused the dismissal. If the subordinate has broken a company rule or refused to change a negative behavior, give specific examples of circumstances that have resulted in his dismissal. If external circumstances, such as budget cutbacks, are the cause, explain those details to your subordinate.

Give the effective date of dismissal

If an employee is being dismissed because of behavioral issues, the dismissal is likely to be immediate. If external circumstances cause the dismissal, the employee might have several weeks before the dismissal becomes effective. Be sure that your subordinate has a clear understanding of the effective date of his dismissal to eliminate misunderstandings and to legally protect your organization.

Provide details about the dismissal

Give your subordinate information about picking up his final paycheck. If the subordinate's job required the use of company property, determine when and how that property will be returned to your organization. If an exit interview is required of the subordinate, work with him to schedule it. Provide any additional details that might be pertinent to the subordinate's dismissal.

Offer positive measures that might be taken on the subordinate's behalf

If your subordinate is dismissed due to external circumstances, you might be able to offer your recommendation and other placement assistance. If the employee is eligible for any severance pay or salary for unused vacation, be sure to obtain that information to facilitate an easier transition. If there is a possibility of the employee being rehired by your company in future, give the employee those details as well.

Provide an official written notice of dismissal

Given that communicating about a dismissal is often emotional, providing the employee with an official written notice is important. It will serve as a reference to the details of the dismissal. It also offers an opportunity to be more in-depth regarding benefits programs and severance pay. Finally, the written notice of dismissal can also serve an important legal function if any dispute should arise between the dismissed employee and the organization.

Do it!

B-2:   Dismissing an employee

Exercise

1 Read the following conversation. Then place it in the proper order according to the guidelines for dismissing an employee.

In compliance with the legal rules and regulations, your lay off will take effect as of August 20th.

Martha, thanks for coming into the meeting. Unfortunately, I have an important task to carry out, one which I am not happy about. Because of the ongoing recession in the IT industry, we have decided to take certain steps to cut costs, including reducing our workforce.

It is not that you are being singled out. The axe is going to fall on 300 people in our organization. The HR department will give you your paycheck on your last working day.

This is a written notice of your layoff. Let me also add that I would really like to have you continue working for me, but there isn't much that I can do.

I know of certain placement organizations that will be able to help you find another job, given the skill set that you have. Here are their addresses.

Unit summary: Colleagues and subordinates

Topic A   In this unit, you learned about the **guidelines for communicating with colleagues.** You also learned how to **present your ideas to your colleagues** and how to **respond to your colleagues' ideas.**

Topic B   Finally, you learned about how best to **apologize to a subordinate.** You then learned about the appropriate tactics for **refusing a subordinate's request.** You also learned about how to **dismiss a subordinate.**

Independent practice activity

1   What are the guidelines for communicating with your colleagues?

2   How should you respond to a colleague's idea?

3   Which of the following steps should you follow when apologizing to your subordinates?

   A   Propose and explain solutions.

   B   Listen to those who have been affected by your error.

   C   Start implementing the solution before you apologize.

   D   Offer a sincere apology.

   E   Don't admit fault or accept blame.

   F   Assess the error and the damage that has been caused.

4   Whether you support or disagree with a colleague's idea, it is important to keep your feedback positive and specific.

   A   True

   B   False

5   If an employee is being dismissed because of an external factor, the dismissal is likely to be immediate.

   A   True

   B   False

Unit 6

Customers and vendors

Unit time: 30 minutes

Complete this unit, and you'll know how to:

A Respond to customers' complaints.

B Reject a vendor's contract without rejecting the vendor and address a complaint to a vendor.

Topic A: Communicating with customers

Explanation

Your customers include anyone who uses your company or organization to obtain goods and services. Customers might be internal or external. An internal customer is a member of your organization and can be a supervisor, colleague, or subordinate. An external customer is someone from outside your organization. Each customer is of equal importance, regardless of the amount of business that customer provides to your organization. You should provide the same level of quality goods and services all your customers, and all are equally deserving of efficient and effective communication.

Communicating with customers is an on-going process. First of all, you need to communicate with potential customers to build an external customer base. Once you have established this base, you must maintain contact with your customers to ensure that you continue to meet their needs. The true test of a successful business is not the number of customers you can attract, but your ability to retain satisfied customers. If a customer becomes dissatisfied with your company, you must communicate a desire to work with that customer to resolve the problem.

Ways of communicating

The type of communication used with a customer should always be adapted to the situation. Face-to-face communication is generally the best form of communication with customers because it allows both you and the customer to read and interpret verbal and nonverbal cues, which might be lost in other forms of communication, such as a telephone call or an e-mail.

In certain situations, a phone call is obviously going be the most appropriate form of communication. For example, if a repeat customer seeks a specific piece of information, such as the speed or capabilities of a particular product your company sells, it would be appropriate to call that customer with the information. However, if your customer has no prior knowledge of your product line, the best solution is probably to schedule an appointment, so that you can visit the customer in person to demonstrate your products.

Responding to customer complaints

Unfortunately, problems do occur in business. Products break or do not live up to expectations. Employees mistreat a customer. The manner in which these situations are handled can make or break a company. To effectively respond to customer complaints, you should follow these five steps:

1   Obtain all pertinent information.
2   Confirm the problem.
3   Express empathy.
4   Develop a solution.
5   Follow up.

Obtain all pertinent information

You cannot solve the problem if you do not understand the details of the situation. Ask the customer to clearly explain the situation. It is important to realize that the customer might need to express her anger, and it is equally important to react calmly rather than defensively. Allow the customer to explain as much as she can about the situation.

Confirm the problem

Once you believe that you have all the facts, confirm your understanding of the problem by repeating or paraphrasing what the customer has told you. You do not need to admit fault or accept blame, but instead acknowledge that an error has occurred and that you are going to work with the customer toward a solution.

Express empathy

It is important to acknowledge the customer's frustration when a problem has occurred. Express empathy for the customer by saying something such as, "We're sorry that this problem has occurred." This approach serves not as an acceptance of fault but as a response to the customer's situation.

Develop a solution

If there is an apparent solution to the customer's problem, explain the solution to the customer. Discuss what steps you'll take and what steps the customer must take to solve the problem. In addition, provide any additional information the customer needs to solve the problem.

If a solution is not apparent, explain to the customer how a solution will be developed. If the customer needs to work with anyone else in your organization to develop a solution, identify those people. Give the customer an idea of what to expect as your organization works toward a resolution. Finally, you need to document the agreed upon solution for both the customer and your company.

Follow up

How your company responds after a complaint has been made is as important as how your company responds to the complaint. If promises are made to the customer and are not fulfilled, the customer is not likely to do business with your company in the future. Follow the documented solution that was developed with the customer, and if possible, go beyond what is expected. If you are able to provide the customer with more than she expects, that customer is more likely to return to your company for future needs. Within a reasonable amount of time, check back with the customer to confirm that the solution has been implemented and that the customer is satisfied with it.

A-1: Responding to complaints

Exercises

1 Watch the movie clip and then answer the following questions.

Was Julia able to develop a
solution to Ms. Dawson's
problem?

Did she identify someone who
could help Ms. Dawson? Why?

2 In the following scene, Laurie McMillan is making a follow up call.

Laurie: Hello, this is Laurie McMillan from Icon International. I'd like to speak with Mr. Carr please.

Laurie: Hello, Mr. Carr, I'm calling on behalf of Shelly Neal to make sure your replacement order was delivered, and to answer any questions you might have.

Laurie: Yes, the brochures list our 24-hour, toll-free service number and our website address, so if anyone needs help, they'll be able to contact us right away.

Laurie: Well, I'm glad to hear that. I hope it will be helpful. Don't hesitate to call me if you have any more questions. Goodbye Mr. Carr.

Now, discuss the following:

Did Laurie make sure that Mr.
Carr's needs were met? How?

3 Place the following steps for responding to customer complaints in proper order.

Develop a solution

Confirm the problem

Obtain all pertinent information

Express empathy

Follow up

4 You receive a call from an annoyed customer. The product that the customer purchased is not compatible with a computer. You know that if an additional driver worth $25 is installed, the product can be made compatible.

How well did the performing student handle the complaint?

Did the student follow the steps for responding to customer complaints?

5 Your instructor will choose two students to enact the following situation.

You have ordered a video camera that is compatible with a computer. You went on vacation and used the camera extensively. When you plugged the video camera into your computer, you received an error message: "Not compatible". You call the vendor to discuss your problem.

How did the student who played the vendor respond to the customer's complaint?

Topic B: Communicating with vendors

Explanation

A vendor is anyone outside your company who provides it with goods or services. Examples of vendors might include office supply providers, janitorial services, and corporate trainers, as well as vendors who provide your company with the necessary raw materials for your products. Having good working relationships with your vendors is important because they have goods or services on which your organization relies.

It is important to build vendor relationships from the start of your organization. You need to communicate with potential vendors about your organization's goals, plans, needs, and desires. Encourage potential vendors to submit bids for their goods or services. Once you have selected a vendor, communicate acceptance of that vendor's bid in writing. Create a contract listing the goods, services, prices, and any additional conditions that you've established with the vendor.

Once you have established a relationship with a vendor, regular communication with the vendor is vital. Maintaining communication with the vendor allows you to immediately address any concerns or problems that occur. In addition, regular contact gives your organization an opportunity to provide the vendor with positive feedback, which helps build a sense of teamwork between the vendor and your organization.

Rejecting a vendor's contract proposal

Rejecting a contract proposal is always difficult. The key to rejecting a contract proposal without alienating the vendor is to focus the rejection on the contract itself and not on any external or personal issues. Your goal is to maintain open communication with the vendor because even though the vendor did not win this particular contract, you might want to do business with this vendor in the future.

When informing a vendor that his contract proposal has been rejected, focus on the positive aspects of the situation. Mention what was good about the proposal before explaining what factors caused the contract to be denied. Thank the vendor for submitting the contract proposal, and express an interest in doing business with him at a later date.

Do it!

B-1: Rejecting a vendor's proposal

Exercises

1 Watch the movie clip and then answer the following questions.

   Was Benjamin able to reject the
   proposal?

   Did he reject the vendor as well?

2 Identify the actions that will enable you to properly reject a vendor's contract.

   A   Express interest in doing future business

   B   Focus on positive aspects

   C   Explain good points first

   D   Thank vendor for submission of contract

   E   Send a form letter rejecting the contract

   F   Tell vendor the problems with the contract first

   G   Ask vendor to change contract

Complaining to a vendor

Explanation

Occasionally, you'll accept a contract but find that you are dissatisfied with the goods or services received. If this situation occurs, follow these three steps to complain effectively to your vendor:

   1   Give facts to explain the problem.

   2   Propose or ask for a solution.

   3   Affirm a desire to work with the vendor toward a mutual solution.

Give facts to explain the problem

Do not let your emotions cloud your abilities to state the facts of the situation. Clearly explain to the vendor what you expected and what actually occurred. Give specific details such as the date or frequency of the problem. If you can quantify the problem in terms of lost hours or financial losses, offer those numbers to the vendor.

Propose or ask for a solution

If you have a specific solution in mind, share it with the vendor. If you do not have a proposed solution, ask the vendor to formulate one. Let the vendor know that you are willing to compromise to work toward a solution, but make it clear that you won't settle for less than the terms of your original contract.

Affirm a desire to work with the vendor toward a mutual solution

Finish the complaint by affirming your commitment to cooperate with the vendor through positive language. Use "we" rather than "I" or "you" to affirm that you want to work with, not against, the vendor. Build a spirit of teamwork to find a solution that is mutually acceptable.

Do it!

B-2: Complaining to a vendor

1 Place the following steps for complaining to a vendor in the proper order.

Affirm a desire to work with the
vendor for a mutual solution

Give facts to explain the problem

Propose or ask for a solution

2 **First meeting:** The Quality Control Manager has to meet with the Purchasing Manager for East Coast Mariner's Supply, a customer. ECMS is the primary distributor of Icon's new WL Global Positioning System. The Purchasing Manager has received numerous complaints about the LCD panel of the 20-20 model. The Quality Control Manager has agreed to meet with the Purchasing Manager to handle the complaint. When in use, the LCD panels sometimes have several white, red, green, or blue dots on them that remain on the panel's surface. These dots are called dead or stuck pixels. This problem is most likely an issue with the LCD panel itself. Replacing or refurbishing the panel can correct the pixel problem.

Objective of this meeting: The Quality Control Manager needs to handle the customer's complaint effectively.

Second meeting: The Quality Control Manager has to meet with a vendor for Atlas Technological Products. Atlas is supplying the department with faulty LCD panels. Icon's contract with Atlas for the LCD panels in question states that the panels will have no more than three dead or stuck pixels per panel.

Objective of this meeting: The Quality Control Manager must effectively present the complaints to the vendor in order to find a solution to the problem.

The Purchasing Manager is a straightforward individual who is practical and patient for the most part. This customer is friendly and easy-going, and attends to business in a professional and conscientious manner. The Purchasing Manager only becomes upset if legitimate concerns are not being addressed.

The vendor is a confident individual with an outgoing personality. This vendor will go out of the way to accommodate clients and co-workers. However, the vendor is tough and demands to know the details of every transaction in which he or she is involved. If not satisfied, the vendor will not proceed.

Was the Quality Control Manager able to handle the Purchasing Manager's complaint effectively?

Was the Quality Control Manager able to effectively present the complaints to the vendor?

What went wrong during the first meeting?

What went wrong during the second meeting?

Unit summary: Customers and vendors

Topic A   In this unit, you learned about the **different ways of communicating with customers** and about **responding to customer complaints**.

Topic B   Finally, you learned about **rejecting a vendor's contract without rejecting the vendor** and the steps for **complaining effectively to your vendors**.

Independent practice activity

1   Which of the following actions will enable you to properly reject a vendor's contract.

   A   Do not give reasons for the rejection

   B   Express disinterest in future business

   C   Express interest in doing future business

   D   Thank vendor for submission of contract

   E   Explain good points first

   F   Send a form letter rejecting the contract

   G   Focus on positive aspects

2   Which communication method would you use if you were seeking a specific piece of information?

   A   Face-to-face

   B   Phone call

3   When responding to a customer complaint, you have obtained all pertinent information. What should you do next?

   A   Express empathy

   B   Develop a solution

   C   Confirm the problem

   D   Follow up

4   The key to rejecting a contract proposal without alienating the vendor is to focus the rejection on the contract and not on any external or personal issues.

   A   True

   B   False

Unit 7

Organizational culture

Unit time: 80 minutes

Complete this unit, and you'll know how to:

A Determine the nature of an organization's culture.

B Use the cultural network to your advantage and identify the characteristics of the roles exhibited in the network.

C Identify the elements of physical culture that affect interpersonal communication.

D Identify the ways in which managers can build a positive culture.

Topic A: Understanding organizational cultures

Explanation

An *organizational culture* is the personality of an organization. This personality is both determined and accepted by the organization's members. For example, an organization might have a culture that is youthful, energetic, and fast-paced. In this type of culture, decisions are made quickly and employees are empowered to take action in a wide variety of situations. Another organization might be more straight-laced and policy-oriented. This organization would much more formal and serious in the way it does business. It is important to recognize and understand the culture of an organization so that you can determine your fit with the organization.

Organizational cultures are relatively stable throughout the course of an organization's lifetime. A certain amount of evolution of the organizational culture occurs as society progresses and changes; however, the culture itself will probably not change radically without a correspondingly radical change in organization's size or structure. Every occupation has an organizational culture. The type of occupation, such as hospitality, manufacturing, or banking, helps determine the culture. For example, the culture in a fast-food restaurant that typically employs high school and college students is different than the culture at an accounting firm. Within an occupation, culture will be determined by the size of the organization, as well as by the philosophy of the management or directors.

Every person employed by an organization is an important part of that organization's culture. An employee is both affected by the culture and plays an integral part in directing the organization's culture. Employees affect the culture by bringing their personal experiences and perspectives to the job. For example, optimistic people who are usually happy tend to cheer those around them, which creates a more positive culture for the entire organization. At the same time, an organizational culture might affect employees by directing them to act in a way that is acceptable within the culture. For example, an employee who is laid-back and casual might act more formally to match the culture of a more formal organization.

An organizational culture begins at the start of the organization and is influenced by the people who created it. Each person involved in creating an organization brings a variety of experiences, preferences, and perceptions to the organization, each of which affects the culture. From that starting point, as employees are chosen, organizational philosophies are put in writing, locations are determined, and the culture is shaped into a combination of each person's personality.

Newcomers to an organization can be socialized both formally and informally. Many organizations arrange for newcomers to have a mentor for their first several weeks on the job. Newcomers might have a question-and-answer session with their mentor to teach them about the culture, or they might acclimate themselves to the culture by mimicking the mentor's actions. New employees can also learn about the culture's characteristics by reading an employee handbook or simply by observation. In some cultures, an initiation ritual might take place. For example, an informal organization might play a joke on a newcomer in order to initiate that person into the organization's humorous culture.

Understanding organizational cultures is important because culture affects the communication within an organization. Understanding organizational culture helps communication flow between employees, departments, or divisions. A significant aspect of communication within an organizational culture is job satisfaction. As a potential employee of an organization, it is important that you understand the culture in order to determine how well you fit in. If you prefer a work environment that promotes regular sharing of ideas among employees, you might not be satisfied working in a culture that encourages autonomy. As a result of job dissatisfaction, communication might falter or break down, causing negative effects for both the employee and the organization. Therefore, determining an organization's culture is enables you to in minimize job dissatisfaction and communication failures.

Do it!

A-1: Adjusting to the organizational culture

Exercises

1 In the following scene, Phyllis (supervisor), Chris (new employee), and Nicholas (supervisor) are seated at the table in Nicholas's office. There are day planners and folders on the table.

Phyllis: Chris, I'd like you to meet Nicholas. Nicholas is a senior sales representative who has been with Icon for six years.

Chris: Nice to meet you, Nicholas.

Nicholas: Nice to meet you, too.

Phyllis: Nicholas is going to be your mentor for the first three weeks here at Icon. He'll be the person you go to if you have any questions or need any help with anything as you get settled in.

Chris: Sounds great.

Nicholas: I've cleared my schedule for this morning, so I can take you on a tour of the company and get you settled into your office. Should we get started?

What did Phyllis do to help the new employee socialize to the new culture?

What are the other ways in which you can help new employees adjust to the new culture?

What kind of culture does this organization demonstrate?

2 Below are the images of reception area of two organizations. Which of the offices would you prefer to work for? Why?

Office 1

Office 2

Elements of an organizational culture

Explanation

Organizational cultures vary, even within the same occupation. Several elements distinguish one culture from another:

- Amiability
- Job autonomy
- Degree of structure
- Recognition and rewards
- Opportunities for personal growth
- Tolerance of risk and change
- Response to concerns

Amiability

The amount of social interaction among employees determines an organization's *amiability*. Some organizations consider themselves a "family," while other organizations might be less social as a result of physical or emotional distance. You can determine the amiability of an organization by asking about social functions such as parties and celebrations.

Job autonomy

Some organizations might encourage a great deal of autonomy, while others prefer or require their employees to interact with each other consistently. For example, a hotel employee with a high degree of autonomy might be empowered to provide a discount to a customer who was dissatisfied with the accommodations. Conversely, a newspaper columnist who submits her column to an editor for review would have less autonomy because she must rely on her co-workers to complete her job. The type of occupation might direct the degree of autonomy, but it is also often directed by the organization's philosophy. You can determine job autonomy by asking managers and co-workers to explain how much interaction with other employees your job requires.

Degree of structure

The *degree of structure* in an organization can be determined by considering the number of written and recorded policies the organization has in place. Organizations with a high degree of structure will likely present new employees with a large handbook covering everything from dress codes to benefits. An organization with a low degree of structure might or might not offer new employees a handbook and might not have many documented procedures. To determine the degree of structure in an organization, you can ask managers or co-workers to explain how policies are formulated or documented.

Recognition and rewards

Recognition and rewards play an important part in job satisfaction. Most people welcome and thrive on praise and acknowledgement of a job well done. It is important to ask about the frequency of recognition and requirements for rewards when taking on a position in a new company.

Opportunities for personal growth

Some organizational cultures encourage employees to expand their knowledge and experiences. This might include offering management training programs or tuition reimbursement for employees working toward a degree. Other organizational cultures are concerned about whether their employees perform their tasks at a specific time and in a specific manner. Before taking a new position, you should ask about the opportunities for personal growth and to determine if the organization's views on personal growth match your own.

Tolerance of risk and change

While some organizations encourage well-planned risk and change, others focus on tradition and stability. You can ask managers or co-workers to explain the company's position on risk and change before accepting a position in order to determine whether the organization's values match your own.

Response to concerns

Although every organization probably considers itself adequate at responding to employee concerns, you should determine whether your concerns would be met according to your expectations. You can ask co-workers or managers to explain the company's philosophy on seeking out and responding to employee concerns. If possible, have someone describe a situation where a concern was presented and how the organization responded. Consider whether the response seemed genuine and effective, and determine whether the company's response matches your own criteria for responding to employee concerns.

Do it!

A-2: Discussing elements of organizational culture

Exercises

1 In the following scene, Chris (subordinate) and Nicholas (supervisor) are seated at the table in Nicholas's office. There are day planners and folders on the table.

Nicholas: Chris, have you received a copy of the employee handbook yet?

Chris: No, I haven't.

Nicholas: Okay, here's a copy for you. Because we belong to such a large company, it's important to have a lot of procedures in place, so everybody knows what rules to follow.

Chris: Wow, that's a big book.

Nicholas: I know it looks like a lot, but it's nothing you need to memorize. Just read through it and let me know if you have any questions. You can keep the book in your office for reference.

What element of organizational culture is shown here?

What is the importance of a handbook?

2 Which of the following is an element of organization's internal culture?

A Motivation

B Resource allocation

C Job autonomy

D Cooperation among departments

3 Which of the following is an element of an organization's internal culture?

A Strength of administration

B Resource allocation

C Tolerance of diversity

D Opportunities for personal growth

Characteristics of a positive organizational culture

Explanation

There are five characteristics that positive organizational cultures have in common:

- Shared philosophy
- Clear direction and focus
- Emphasis on employees
- Heroes
- Rituals and ceremonies

Shared philosophy

Each positive organizational culture has a *shared philosophy*. This philosophy explains the culture, vision, and importance of the organization to the industry, its employees, and the community. The philosophy is usually written; however, in smaller organizations all employees might simply understand it. A shared philosophy bands people together to work towards a common goal.

Clear direction and focus

Positive organizational cultures also have a clear direction and focus. A positive culture has one or several strong leaders who continually guide the organization toward the focus. As with a philosophy, the direction and focus might be formally distributed or might simply be understood by employees. An organization's direction and focus might be displayed on a wall as a vision statement, or it might be passed on informally, such as by repeating it at each staff meeting. Regardless of how the message is perpetuated, the focus must be clear and understood by employees at every level of the organization.

Emphasis on employees

Organizations with positive cultures make their employees a priority. Strong cultures are known for taking care of employees through competitive salaries and fair benefits. In addition, there is an informal emphasis on employees when leaders interact and socialize with employees regularly. This interaction helps employees feel that the leaders place value on getting to know them.

Heroes

Positive organizational cultures also have *heroes,* whose efforts are either historical or remarkable. Historical heroes are the founders of an organization who typically overcame adversity to make the organization successful. Remarkable heroes are leaders who achieved greatness through success, such as an account executive who set a record for the most new accounts in a month. The stories of heroes are told and retold as employees come into an organization and learn about the company's history. Heroes help provide continuity with the organization's past, and repeating their stories make employees feel more a part of the organization.

Rituals and ceremonies

Rituals and ceremonies are an important aspect of any positive organizational culture because they make the organization seem more personable to its employees. Rituals and ceremonies include birthday celebrations, recognition banquets, or even weekly meetings. As with stories of the company' heroes, rituals and ceremonies help new employees feel more a part of the organization's culture.

Do it!

A-3: Identifying organizational culture

Exercises

1 In the following scene, Phyllis (supervisor), Valerie (subordinate), and Matt (subordinate) are seated at the table in the conference room.

Phyllis: Thanks for coming to our monthly recognition meeting. Valerie, would you like to go first with the birthdays?

Valerie: This month we're honoring Sue and Jim. Sue's birthday was the 12th, and Jim's birthday will be on the 25th.

Phyllis: Thank you, Valerie.

Phyllis: Matt, I'll turn things over to you for the awards announcement.

Matt: Thanks, Phyllis. This month we have several awards to present. Let me first mention the awards that were won at the annual trade show last weekend, and then I'll present the Employee of the Month.

Does the discussion depict a
positive organizational culture?

What are the characteristics of a positive organizational culture?

2 Read the following scenarios and identify the characteristic that the organizational
culture reflects.

Our people are always on the
move. Do you know that every
morning and evening flight across
the world has at least one of our
employees on it?

Have you heard of the member of
the housekeeping staff who found
a briefcase a customer left after
the customer checked out? The
staff member went to the airport
to find out where the customer
was going next. The staff member
boarded the next flight for the
same destination and delivered the
briefcase to that customer. The
customer never ever thought of
going to another hotel.

We got a complaint at 4:30 p.m.
from the stock exchange. We'd
installed our equipment in the
there. It was vital for the customer
to get the problem fixed by 8:00
a.m. next day before the trading
hours began. A 30-member team
flew down to the premises from
across the country to rectify the
problem. The system was up and
running by 5:00 a.m.

3 Pat has to meet two team leaders from Icon's Market Research department. The Industrial Services and Manufacturing division is redefining its culture and has asked for inputs and suggestions from each department.

Pat has to lead this meeting and identify the areas of culture that can be changed or improved to make a more efficient and productive culture.

The first team leader is a friendly individual who genuinely cares about the company's overall performance. This person is not overly ambitious, but tries to help whenever possible and is frequently the first person to notice when there's a problem.

The second team leader has an easygoing attitude and is therefore enthusiastic about new situations. This person is usually very friendly and open, but can become too attached to issues of personal interest and concern. The second team leader is very protective of their work and likes to make sure there's time to cover all concerns.

Was Pat able to identify the areas of culture that can be changed or improved?

Topic B: Cultural networks

Explanation

A *cultural network* is a combination of the formal and informal hierarchy and communication channels within an organization. It is through the cultural network that the elements of a culture are transmitted, reinforced, and blended into a culture that is unique to each organization.

As with a regional or national culture, language connects people in an organizational culture. A shared language includes words and phrases that are specific to that occupation and organization, including acronyms and jargon. This shared language unites the people within that culture by giving the members a sense of belonging.

An organization's culture is often perpetuated through storytelling. Storytelling might be a formal statement of the company's history or an informal spoken account of corporate heroes and legends. Storytelling reinforces the organization's beliefs and values and enables employees to share those beliefs and values with others in the organization. As information is dispersed through communication, the culture is perpetuated.

Using cultural networks

The cultural network within an organization is used to distribute information. Sometimes it is used deliberately as messages are sent through a formal hierarchy. For example, the company president might write a memo and give it to her secretary, who e-mails the memo to each of the organization's team leaders. Each team leader then e-mails his or her team members to share the information in the memo.

Information might also be spread informally throughout the cultural network. For example, if an employee resigns to take a job with a competitor, that information might be dispersed via informal channels before an official announcement is made. Often, personal information or information that affects a wide range of employees spreads faster through informal channels than through the formal hierarchy. When considering the most efficient way to dispense information in an organization, it is important to consider the time frame, priority, and details of the message to be sent in order to best take advantage of the cultural network.

Advantages of cultural networks

There are several advantages of using a cultural network to disseminate information. One advantage is that because the information is contained within the organization, there is no outside contamination of the information. Another advantage is that the information will probably be transmitted using words and terms that are familiar to all recipients because, as a part of the organizational culture, they are familiar with the shared language. Also, the cultural network allows for information to be transmitted to all members of the network, regardless of status.

Disadvantages of cultural networks

The disadvantages of using the cultural network include decreased productivity and decreased integrity of information. Decreased productivity can result when vague information is passed through the cultural network. If information is vague or unclear, employees have to spend time clarifying, verifying, and analyzing the information.

Decreased integrity of information is a concern whenever information is passed informally through the cultural network. When information is passed informally, it can be altered slightly by each person who passes it on. As the information spreads through the cultural network, it can evolve into a form that barely resembles the original information. To counteract the effects of decreased productivity and integrity, make sure you give clear and specific facts whenever you use the cultural network.

Do it!   ## B-1:   Using cultural networks

Multiple-choice questions

1 Which of the following connects people in an organizational culture?

A   Literature

B   Commitment

C   Common backgrounds

D   Language

2 Which of the following is an advantage of using an organization's cultural network to distribute information?

A   Familiarity of terms

B   Specific distribution

C   Impurity of information

D   Guaranteed receptiveness

3 Which of the following is a disadvantage of using an organization's cultural network to distribute information?

A   Increased integrity of information

B   Decreased integrity of information

C   Increased productivity

D   Increased flow of communication

4 As a member of an organization, you'll use its cultural network to distribute information. Which of the following is an advantage of using an organization's cultural network to distribute information?

A   Purity of information

B   Accuracy of timing

C   Nobility of purpose

D   Guaranteed communication

Roles within the cultural network

Explanation

Each employee plays a role within a cultural network. That role is determined by both the individual's personality and the need for balance within an organization. Almost every organization will have a balance of individuals in the following roles:

- Narrators
- Guardians
- Anonymous Powers
- Gossipmongers
- Clerical Sources
- Secret Agents
- Alliances

Narrators

Narrators seek power and influence by interpreting and repeating the activities that take place in an organization. Narrators perpetuate the culture of an organization through stories of corporate heroes and legends. A drawback of learning about the organization's culture from a narrator is that his stories comprise his perceptions, rather than a factual account of events. To be an effective narrator, the employee must have an eye for detail as well as an imagination to turn those details into a story. Narrators enjoy the drama and power of their roles. If you find yourself using a narrator to disperse information in a cultural network, it is important to make the narrator feel important and to play to his desire for drama.

Guardians

Guardians are the caretakers of an organization. They are most often mature, responsible, and well-respected mid- to high-level managers. Guardians are accessible to listen and offer solutions to any problem, whether professional or personal. When using guardians to disperse information in a cultural network, appeal to their sense of commitment to the well being of the organization. When guardians feel responsible for an action within their organization, nothing will take a greater priority.

Anonymous powers

Anonymous powers are influential people who might not outwardly hold a position of power within the organization. An employee who has anonymous power has a close relationship with the apparent power, such as a company president or chief executive officer. In addition, the anonymous power has a strong network of contacts throughout the organization. Because of these contacts, the anonymous power knows what goes on behind the scenes in an organization. An anonymous power is especially effective in dispensing information to people in the organization's high-level roles because the anonymous power influence those people.

Gossipmongers

Gossipmongers, like narrators, are very detail-oriented. The difference, however, is that narrators weave details into stories to be shared when they are most effective, whereas gossipmongers take those details and embellishes them before dispersing them. They do so purely for entertainment. Gossipmongers cannot be expected to be serious or factual, so you should not disperse any important information through them.

Clerical Sources

Clerical sources are an important part of the cultural network because they are a relatively unbiased source of information. Clerical sources are often the most informed people regarding the activities within an organization and are in the unique position of being able to transmit information to all levels of the cultural network. For example, clerical sources can dispense information from upper levels of management throughout the organization. In addition, clerical sources can share information from other clerical and lower-level employees with high-level managers. Because other roles can be effective in dispensing information from upper management throughout an organization, the clerical source is most valuable when dispensing information upward from lower-level employees.

Secret agents

Secret agents are employees within a cultural network who are extremely loyal to a person in a position of power. Secret agents are well liked by other employees, which makes it easy for them to gather information and maintain an unbiased perspective of events in the workplace. The person in a position of power to whom the secret agent is loyal often sets aside time for the secret agent to share insights and perceptions. While other roles in the cultural network are used most often for dispensing information, the secret agent's primary role is to provide insights and perceptions. As a result, you would use the secret agent to receive information rather than to dispense it throughout the organization.

Alliances

An *alliance* occurs when two or more people secretly join together for a common purpose, which is usually advancement within the organization. The members of an alliance share a deep bond of trust and support for one another. Alliances are an important part of the cultural network because an alliance member will rapidly dispense any information she has to other members of the alliance. While this can work to your advantage, it is important to avoid dispensing information through an alliance when it is important that all employees receive the information in the same time frame.

Do it!

B-2: Discussing roles in cultural networks

Exercises

1 Watch the movie clip and then answer the following questions.

   What kind of role is Nicholas
   exhibiting?

   What are the characteristics of this role?

2 In the following scene, Benjamin (supervisor) and Laurie (subordinate) are seated at the table in Benjamin's office. There are day planners and folders on the table.

   Benjamin: Laurie, I know that everyone here at Icon likes you and enjoys talking with you. I wondered if you've heard anything, good or bad, about the memo that went out last week?

   Laurie: Actually, I've heard several positive comments. The only concern I've heard anyone mention involves the vacation request policy. Several people are concerned that it will change.

   Benjamin: I was afraid that mentioning it in the memo with the other changes might make it sound that way. I'll send out another memo to clarify that. Thanks, Laurie.

   What role does Laurie play in the
   given situation?

   What are the characteristics of people performing this role?

3 Match each set of characteristics listed below to one of the following roles: clerical sources, alliances, anonymous powers, gossipmongers, and narrators.

Like to embellish details

Have close relationships with apparent powers

Tell stories

Two or more people joined together for a common purpose

Most helpful when dispensing information upward

4 Which of the following is a characteristic of a guardian?

A   Caretakers of an organization

B   Extremely loyal to a person in a position of power

C   Like to embellish details

D   Have a close relationship with an apparent power

5 Pat has to meet with a supervisor from the Receiving department. This supervisor has been recently transferred from Icon's Chicago division, and has had a difficult time adjusting to the cultural network in the Boston office.

Pat has to discuss the cultural network and make the supervisor feel more comfortable with the communication process. Pat should explain the communication process and make suggestions on how the supervisor can improve the effectiveness of communication.

The supervisor has a friendly disposition, a good sense of humor, and a positive attitude. This person sets high goals in work but needs frequent reassurance and encouragement. In times of stress, the supervisor can become emotional and distrustful and has a tendency to offer excuses when confronted with conflict.

How did the discussion go?

Was Pat able to explain the communication process to the supervisor?

What went wrong during their discussion?

Topic C: Managing physical culture

Explanation

Every work environment has a physical culture, which affects the overall organizational culture and the communication that takes place within the culture. If employees perceive themselves as working in a high-quality environment, the efficiency and effectiveness of their work and communication improve. It is also important to recognize a workplace's physical elements to eliminate status issues within that environment. To promote productive meetings, you need to consider the type of space you use for both large and small groups.

Elements of physical culture

The elements of physical culture that affect interpersonal communication include the following:

- Space
- Privacy
- Height
- Proximity
- Ownership
- Cleanliness
- Quality

Space

Generally, the amount of *space* assigned to an employee indicates his or her rank in an organization. A company president usually has a large office, often with a view, while an account executive has a small office or cubicle. Any time there is incongruence between status and space, look closer to see what role the employee fills. He might hold a higher level of power than his job description indicates.

Privacy

The amount of *privacy* an individual has also indicates status. Employees with cubicles or shared offices do not have as much privacy as a higher-ranking employee with her own office. Privacy is important to consider when determining how accessible employees will be. Employees who have their own offices and keep their doors closed are not perceived as open or welcoming, and they might not be able to manage effectively.

Height

Status can be expressed through *height* in two different ways. First, in an organization that occupies several floors of a building, the higher-ranking officials are often located on the higher floors. Second, height also can be a factor when meeting in a private office or conference room. The leader of a meeting will often sit in a chair that is slightly higher than the other chairs in the room. This draws attention to the meeting leader.

Proximity

Proximity is the physical space between two things. It is another indicator of status and can either segregate or unify. It is important to recognize and regulate proximity to reduce or eliminate questions of status.

For example, assigning a manager office space that is distant from the employees he oversees might isolate that manager. Employees will perceive that the manager is too important or too busy to be concerned with their problems, and a breakdown in communication will occur. To eliminate problems with proximity, assign space so that managers and subordinates are close to one another and departments that work together are located in the same area.

Ownership

Ownership is another element of physical culture that affects an employee's perception of status because it is often the higher-ranking employees who have ownership over their personal space and items. Ownership indicates sole usage of space, furniture, and office equipment. Often, lower-ranking employees share tables, chairs, and computers rather than being assigned their own.

Cleanliness

The physical cleanliness of an organization has a dramatic affect on the culture and the communication within a culture because it affects the employees' and outsiders' perceptions of the workplace. A clean environment is synonymous with wealth and power, while a dirty environment often indicates a lack of both financial resources and importance within the industry. Worse yet, an unclean environment can suggest an indifferent attitude—one that often shows up in the quality of the work produced.

Quality

Quality is a somewhat abstract element of the physical space that is determined by the structure of the workspace and the furniture within the environment. High-quality building space and furniture are signs of affluence, which is directly related to the perceptions employees have about their jobs. If the workspace and furniture are perceived as being high quality, employees often feel a sense of purpose and dedication to their jobs that they might not feel in a low-quality environment.

Arranging meeting space for a small group

You need to consider several factors when arranging meeting space for a small group. The actual number of people who will be involved, the topic, and the level of comfort the group has with one another should all be taken into consideration when arranging for a small meeting.

With a group of two, three, or four, including yourself, you should arrange the meeting space around a small round or square table. This will give all persons involved a writing space and a place to put cups or other items.

For the meeting, consider whether you are on opposing sides of the topic of discussion. In any sort of negotiation or bargaining, it is best to seat opposing sides on opposite sides of the table. This arrangement enables you to read subtle nonverbal cues the other people might inadvertently send.

The across-the-table arrangement will be necessary if you have a three or four person group, regardless of whether the parties are in opposition or cooperation with each other. However, if you have a two-person meeting where the parties are cooperating with one another, it is best to seat yourselves either side-by-side or across the table and diagonally from one another. These positions allow each of you plenty of room to spread out and be comfortable while still putting you in close contact with one another.

Arranging meeting space for a large group

With a large meeting, group members will either all be seated at a large table, or only a few members will be seated at a table, while the rest of the group will be seated as an audience. Generally, it is best to avoid the audience situation whenever possible. This arrangement does not allow for all group members to feel as though they are on equal terms with the individuals sitting at the table and might affect the results of a conversation or negotiation.

If all members of a group are seated at a table, the group leader usually sits at one end of the table. The seats at the ends of the table are considered powerful positions and usually evoke more action and involvement from the people in those seats, regardless of their leadership status. This is an important point to consider if you have an employee that you would like to encourage to take a more active role in meetings.

If there is no apparent leader of a group, or if the leader is not particularly dominant, spread the seating equally around the table. If the leader of a group has a dominant personality, it is important to seat the other members of the group closer together to maintain a balance. If group members are equally spread out around the table, there will be little or no unity among them, and the dominant leader will control the meeting.

Do it!

C-1:   Arranging meeting space

Exercises

1 Watch the movie clip and then answer the following questions.

What is happening in the discussion?

What should you consider when arranging space for a small group?

2 In following scene, Benjamin (supervisor) and Laurie (subordinate) are planning the seating arrangements for a meeting with a large group.

Laurie: Everyone is going to be sitting at the table, correct?

Benjamin: That's right. I'm sure everyone will want to take notes on Mr. Dawson's presentation. Seating them at the table will give them a place to write.

Laurie: Okay, are the chairs set up like you want them?

Benjamin: Actually, since Mr. Dawson will be at the head of the table, let's move the chairs back a little bit farther. I assume he'll stand during his presentation, and by moving the rest of the chairs back a bit, it will balance things out somewhat better.

Laurie: That's a good idea. If the rest of the group is sitting closer together, they might not be as intimidated and will be more willing to ask questions.

What is happening in the discussion?

What factors should you consider when arranging space for a large group?

3 Identify which elements of physical culture affect interpersonal communication.

A   Intelligence

B   Acceptance of diversity

C   Enthusiasm

D   Privacy

E   Height

F   Space

Topic D: Managing emotional culture

Explanation

Managers affect elements of a positive emotional culture such as leadership, loyalty, and empowerment. It is the manager's responsibility to set an example for strong leadership and effective management. Managers must show loyalty to their employees if they want their employees to return that loyalty. Managers must also empower employees to learn to do things for themselves in order to keep the workplace strong and efficient.

Managers have an important responsibility to create a supportive climate within an organization's culture. Such a climate is necessary to maintain a strong chain of communication. A supportive climate not only uplifts everyone within the organization but also gives them a sense of belonging and unity, which promotes efficient work and communication. Furthermore, a supportive climate empowers employees to take the initiative in proposing new ideas and creative solutions to problems. Therefore, it is important for managers to design a climate that is helpful and compassionate.

Creating a supportive climate

There are three guidelines for creating a supportive climate:

- Maintain an open-door policy.
- Use positive language.
- Offer support.

Maintain an open-door policy

The most important characteristic of an effective manager is accessibility. Maintaining an open-door policy communicates a desire to help employees work through problems that might arise. In addition, an accessible manager is available to notice and reward positive efforts.

Use positive language

An effective manager uses positive language to promote a supportive climate. Effective managers communicate a spirit of teamwork to their employees and set an example of dedication to the job. Positive language, including "We can" and "We will," sets the tone for a supportive climate.

Offer support

Employees often find their managers willing to listen to problems that arise, but an effective manager demonstrates his or her support by working side by side with employees toward a solution or remedy for a problem. This type of support earns managers loyalty that will be useful in the work environment.

Do it!

D-1:   Using positive language

Exercises

1 In the following scene, Phyllis (supervisor) and Pam (subordinate) are seated at the table in Phyllis's office. There are day planners and folders on the table.

Phyllis: Pam, I want to thank you for coming to me with your concerns.

Pam: You're welcome. I wasn't really sure if coming to you was the right thing to do, or if I should try to handle it myself.

Phyllis: Well, it sounds like you've tried to handle it yourself, and have done a great job, but now I think it's time for us to work together toward a permanent solution. I'm sure we can all come together to work something out.

Did Phyllis encourage Pam?

What is the importance of using positive language?

2 Which of the following is a way in which you can build a positive culture.

A   Use negative language

B   Set goals for employees

C   Offer support

D   Giving directions

Empowering employees

Explanation

It is important to communicate to your employees that they have your trust and empowerment. *Empowerment* is the consent and encouragement to act alone for the betterment of the whole company. Here are three things you can do to empower your employees:

- Encourage creativity.
- Encourage new ideas.
- Encourage initiative.

Encourage creativity

The first step to empowering employees is to encourage creativity. You can encourage creativity by giving employees the freedom to discover or research processes and procedures within your organization. You should also encourage brainstorming about ways to improve processes and procedures. It is important to let employees know that this type of creativity is allowed and encouraged, as long as it does not interfere with their work responsibilities.

Encourage new ideas

The second step to empowering employees is to encourage new ideas. You should let employees know you are always willing to listen to and consider any new ideas they have. If an employee comes to you with a new idea, make time to discuss it and share it with other managers to obtain feedback. Doing so communicates to your employees that you take their ideas seriously.

Encourage initiative

Often, the hardest part of empowering employees is encouraging initiative on their parts. It's easy to encourage employees to be creative or be receptive to their new ideas. However, it can sometimes be difficult for managers to encourage employees to take action on those ideas. One reason might be that managers sometimes wish they had thought of the idea. Managers might also be concerned about how a failed idea will reflect on them. However, it is important to encourage your employees to follow through on their ideas. Stifling initiative will stifle creativity, which will then affect all aspects of the employee's job performance.

Do it!

D-2: Encouraging initiative

Exercises

1 In the following scene, Benjamin (supervisor) and Matt (subordinate) are seated at the table in Benjamin's office. There are day planners and folders on the table.

Benjamin: Matt, I got your idea from the suggestion box. Your plan to reroute internal design jobs through the same channels as the external design jobs sounds like a good one.

Matt: Thanks, Mr. Sullivan. It just seemed to make sense to me, and I know you encourage us to share our ideas.

Benjamin: That's right. I can't honestly predict the success of your idea, but it needs to be investigated. Are you willing to take charge of this project and see what can be done with it? If you'll agree to follow through, I'll give you the green light.

What did Benjamin do to empower Matt?

How does encouraging initiative help an organization?

2 Place the following steps for empowering employees in the proper order.

Encourage new ideas

Encourage initiative

Encourage courage

Encourage commitment

Encourage creativity

3 Pat has to meet two line managers from Icon's Industrial Services and Manufacturing division. They are concerned about the increasingly low morale of their employees. They are having a difficult time keeping their employees motivated and satisfied.

Pat has to offer them advice and suggestions that will make the emotional culture in their departments more positive. Throughout the discussion, Pat should answer their questions and address their concerns.

The first line manager is passive and has a tendency to withhold feelings. This manager is a team player, but sometimes lets a fear of failure stand in the way of success. During disagreements, the first line manager plays the role of peacemaker.

The second line manager is a hard-working individual with an easygoing attitude. This manager is known for patience, determination, and good humor. The second line manager believes there is a way to work out every problem, and only becomes frustrated when the lines of communication break down and progress toward a solution ceases.

Did Pat effectively answer the managers' questions and concerns?

Do you think the discussion helped the two line managers?

Unit summary: Organizational culture

Topic A   In this unit, you learned about the **elements of an organizational culture** and the **characteristics of a positive organizational culture**.

Topic B   Next, you learned about the **advantages and disadvantages** of cultural networks and the **different roles exhibited within the cultural network**.

Topic C   Then, you learned about the **elements of a physical culture** and about how to **arrange meeting space** for small and large groups.

Topic D   Finally, you learned about the **guidelines for creating a supportive culture** and the steps involved in **empowering employees**.

Independent practice activity

1 Which of the following is an element of an organization's internal culture?

   A Amiability

   B Cleanliness

   C Tolerance of diversity

   D Reliability

2 Which of the following are characteristics of a positive organizational culture.

   A Rituals and ceremonies

   B Heroes

   C Clear direction and focus

   D Holiday gatherings

   E Medical benefits

3 Which of the following is an advantage of using an organization's cultural network to distribute information?

   A Information is transmitted in unfamiliar terms

   B Information is transmitted regardless of employee's status

   C Information is transmitted in more technical terms

   D Information is transmitted based on employee's status

4 Which of the following is a disadvantage of using an organization's cultural network to distribute information?

A Increased integrity of information

B Increased productivity

C Decreased productivity

D Coherency of information

5 What is an alliance?

6 Which of the following is a characteristic of anonymous powers?

A Extremely loyal to a person in a position of power

B Caretakers of the organization

C Have a close relationship with an apparent power

D Like to embellish details

7 Which of the following elements of physical culture affect interpersonal communication?

A Language

B Amiability

C Cleanliness

D Height

E Proximity

F Unity

Advanced Interpersonal Communication

Course summary

This summary contains information to help you bring the course to a successful conclusion. Using this information, you will be able to:

A Use the summary text to reinforce what you've learned in class.

B Determine the next courses in this series (if any), as well as any other resources that might help you continue to learn about Advanced Interpersonal Communication.

Topic A: Course summary

Use the following summary text to reinforce what you've learned in class.

Advanced Interpersonal Communication

Unit 1

In this unit, you learned about the **four types of primary communication styles: collaborator, contributor, inquisitor, and director**. You also learned about the corresponding **secondary communications styles** for each of these types. Finally, you learned about the **different verbal and nonverbal** modes of communication.

Unit 2

In this unit, you learned about the **elements that influence a first impression**. Then, you learned about the **guidelines** you should follow for **building rapport and credibility** with others. Finally, you learned about the **types of questions** that you should avoid asking and about the **guidelines for asking questions**.

Unit 3

In this unit, you learned about **verbal and nonverbal forms of feedback** and about how to **use paraphrasing effectively**. Finally, you learned how to provide **positive and constructive feedback** in a business setting.

Unit 4

In this unit, you learned about **five types of ineffective supervisors: bullies, guilt trippers, blamers, dreamers, and emotional volcanoes**. You then learned how to **interact** with these types of supervisors. Finally, you learned about the steps for **negotiating a raise** and **handling a job resignation**.

Unit 5

In this unit, you learned the **guidelines for communicating with colleagues**. You also learned how **to apologize to a subordinate**. Then, you learned about the appropriate tactics for **refusing a subordinate's request**.

Unit 6

In this unit, you learned about the **different ways of communicating with customers** and **responding to customer complaints**. Finally, you learned how to **reject a vendor's contract without rejecting the vendor** and how to **complain effectively to vendors**.

Unit 7

In this unit, you learned about the **elements of an organizational culture** and about the **characteristics of a positive organizational culture**. Next, you learned about the **advantages and disadvantages** of using cultural networks to disseminate information and about the **roles exhibited in the cultural network**. Then, you learned about the **elements of a physical culture** and about **arranging meeting space** for small and large groups. Finally, you learned about the **guidelines for creating a supportive culture** and about the steps involved in **empowering employees**.

Topic B: Continued learning after class

It is impossible to learn to use any subject effectively in a single day. To get the most out of this class, it is important that you begin applying the guidelines for effective interpersonal communication as soon as possible. We also offer resources for continued learning.

Next courses in this series

This is the only course in this series.

Other resources

For more information, visit www.axzopress.com.

Glossary

Blamer

A type of supervisor who responds with blame when errors are discovered.

Bully

A type of supervisor who basks in his own authority and uses body, such as crossed arms and peering over eyeglasses, to suggest superiority.

Colleagues

People in your office, team, department, or division who do not hold a supervisory position over you, nor do you hold a supervisory position over them.

Credibility

Respect for and belief in a speaker. A speaker must have credibility to ensure that her message is understood correctly.

Cultural network

A combination of the formal and informal hierarchy and communication channels within an organization.

Customer

Anyone who uses your company or organization to obtain goods and services.

Dreamer

A type of supervisor who has many ideas and complete confidence in herself.

Emotional volcano

A type of supervisor who reacts to fear and frustration through yelling, ranting, and fist pounding.

Guilt tripper

A type of supervisor who uses guilt trips to motivate employees.

Nonverbal feedback

Feedback in the form of a nod or shake of the head, a hand gesture, a questioning expression, or simply silence.

Organizational culture

The personality of an organization. This personality is both determined and accepted by members of the organization.

Paraphrasing

The act of receiving a message, processing it, changing the language, and repeating it to ensure that you comprehend the intended message.

Pitch

The highness or lowness of your voice. When your vocal muscles are taut, your voice has a high pitch; when your vocal muscles are relaxed, your voice has a low pitch.

Rapport

A relationship of mutual trust. In any relationship, it is necessary for you to gain and maintain a sense of trust in order to communicate freely with one another.

Rate

The speed with which you speak.

Subordinate

Anyone who might look to you for guidance, work assignments, salary increases, promotions, or other assistance in the workplace.

Vendor

Anyone outside your company who provides your company with goods or services.

Verbal feedback

The words and phrases used when responding to others. Verbal feedback might be a detailed answer to a question or a simple "yes" or "no."

Index